Books in the **Today's Heroes** Series

DAVE JOHNSON

by Dave Johnson
with Verne Becker

ZondervanPublishingHouse
Grand Rapids, Michigan

A Division of HarperCollinsPublishers

Dave Johnson
Copyright © 1994 by Dave Johnson

Requests for information should be addressed to:
Zondervan Publishing House
Grand Rapids, Michigan 49530

Library of Congress Cataloging-in-Publication Data

Johnson, Dave, 1963–
        Dave Johnson : everyone seemed certain he would
win Olympic gold. Could he meet their expectations—and his
own? / by Dave Johnson with Verne Becker.
        p. cm. – (Today's heroes)
        ISBN 0–310-46181-2 (softcover)
1. Johnson, Dave, 1963–   . 2. Track and field athletes—
United States—Biography. 3. Decathlon. I. Becker, Verne. II.
Title. III. Series: Today's heroes series.
GV697.J64A3 1994b
796.42'092–dc20
[B]
                                                    94-34754
                                                        CIP

Edited by David Lambert and Rachel Boers
Cover design by Mark Veldheer
Cover and interior illustrations by Patrick Kelley

Printed in the United States of America

94 95 96 97 98 99/ ❖ LP /10 9 8 7 6 5 4 3 2 1

Contents

Chronology of Events

April 7, 1963. Dave Johnson is born in Missoula, Montana.

April 1982. As a freshman at Western Oregon State University, Dave competes in his first decathlon, scoring 6297.

April 27, 1984. Dave breaks the 8000 mark in only his sixth decathlon with a first-place score of 8043 in the California Invitational in Pomona.

June 22, 1984. Dave competes in the Olympic Trials in the Los Angeles Coliseum, placing eleventh.

June 19, 1986. At the TAC National Championships in Eugene, Oregon, Dave takes first place with a score of 8203. He is ranked No. 2 in the U.S.

May 1987. During practice, Dave suffers a stress fracture to his right ankle after stepping on a stray shot. Doctors tell him it is a bone spur.

June 12, 1987. Dave marries Sheri Jordan in the little town of Sweet Home, Oregon.

June 24, 1987. As a result of his ankle injury, Dave is forced to withdraw from the TAC National Championships in San Jose, California.

July 21, 1988. Dave wins a spot on the U.S. Olympic Team at the Olympic Trials in Indianapolis, Indiana, with a score of 8245.

September 29, 1988. At the Olympic Games in Seoul, Korea, Dave places ninth with a score of 8180.

June 14, 1989. Dave wins his second U.S. championship in Houston, Texas, posting the world's highest score (8549) for that year. He is ranked first in the U.S. and second in the world.

November 1989. The TAC declares Dave's 8549 score (new javelin) to be a co-American record with Bruce Jenner's 8634 (old javelin). Dave is the first person to touch Jenner's record since 1976.

July 25, 1990. At the Goodwill Games in Seattle, Washington, Dave wins the gold medal with a score of 8403. For the second straight year, he ranks No. 1 in the U.S. and No. 2 in the world.

January 26, 1992. Reebok's "Dan and Dave" TV commercials debut during the Super Bowl.

April 24, 1992. Dave posts his all-time high score of 8727 to win the Mt. SAC Relays in Azusa, California.

June 27, 1992. At the Olympic Trials in New Orleans, Dave takes first place. Dan misses in the pole vault and fails to make the team. Dave reinjures his ankle.

August 6, 1992. Dave wins the bronze medal in the Barcelona Olympic Games after competing on his stress-fractured ankle.

April 13, 1994. After surgery on his ankle in 1992 and a year of recuperation, Dave wins the Mt. SAC Relays, his first decathlon since the Olympics, with a score of 8216. He continues to train full time for the 1996 Games in Atlanta.

1

Seoul Searching

I can't look.

We are pole vaulting at the 1988 Olympic Games in Seoul, Korea. Daley Thompson, two-time gold medalist and decathlon world-record holder, lies stunned in the vaulting pit. On his first attempt at 15'5", his old pole snapped into three pieces with a *thwack*, sending him flailing through the air and—thankfully—into the pads. The crowded stadium falls silent as Daley crawls out, dazed. I think for sure he's hurt himself badly. But other than collecting a few splinters and aggravating an earlier groin injury, he appears to be okay. I breathe a sigh of relief for him. Like a true world-class athlete, he picks up another pole and on his next jump clears the bar easily.

In a way, Daley's vaulting experience sums up his entire performance in the '88 Olympics. Unlike the '80 and '84 games, where he dominated the decathlon, this year he has to struggle through most of the two-day event just to stay in the running for a medal. The world's greatest decathlete is fading, and a new crop of younger competitors, including me, have arrived on the scene. As we stand there watching and warming up, we all know the time has come for a changing of the guard. Who will be the new leader, the new gold medalist?

*　　*　　*

The Seoul Games are by far the largest Olympics ever, with nearly 9,600 athletes competing from 160 countries. From the moment I entered the stadium for the opening ceremonies, my senses were going wild. Everything sent goosebumps running down my arms—the music, the colors, the TV cameras, the march around the track with the world's best athletes, and especially the screaming crowd of thou-

Dave Johnson

sands, all of whom had come to watch *me* compete, or so I thought.

Each time I stepped on that track I checked out the crowd, marveled at all the people, and said to myself, "Man—this is the Olympic Games! This is great—I made it to the Olympic Games!" And the more I talked to myself that way, the more I forgot the task I came there to accomplish—to *win* at the Olympic Games, or at least to do my very best.

There's really no other sport in the world like the decathlon, which means "ten contests." Decathletes must excel in not one but ten different track and field events over two days. On the first day we tackle the 100-meter dash, the long jump, the shot put, the high jump, and the 400 meters; and on the second day we do the 110-meter hurdles, the discus, the pole vault, the javelin, and the 1500 meters. Success in the decathlon requires a lot of things—speed, strength, flexibility, technique, endurance, and more—but it especially requires the ability to focus.

That's the one thing I don't have enough of right now in Seoul. I don't even pray this morning before starting the 100 meters at 9 A.M. The news broke about Ben Johnson yesterday, and it has really cast a shadow over the Olympic

Games. I resolved long ago never to take enhancing drugs, but all the attention the issue is getting distracts me.

The tension before the first event runs extremely high because everyone is so eager to get started. Sometimes guys will throw up out of sheer nervousness. Trying to get myself psyched, I step into the blocks for the 100 meters and pretend I'm Carl Lewis. At the gun, we're off. Pumping my arms and legs, I muster up every bit of energy I've got for this all-out sprint. I try not to look at the runner next to me, but I can feel his presence.

Eleven seconds later (11.15, to be exact) the first event is over. I don't run very close to my personal best, but I do beat the other Americans. I feel a huge sense of relief that I've finally started this thing. Immediately after the race, however, I have to face the most difficult challenge of the decathlon: relaxing between events. You need to forget what time you ran—good or bad—how many points you scored, or how many people are ahead of you. Otherwise you'll use up too much energy either congratulating yourself or getting down on yourself.

The Olympic stadium in Seoul has a locker room under the bleachers with chairs, beds, and sack lunches where the athletes can rest and

Dave Johnson

wait between events. I usually hang out in there and try to nap or relax. I may listen to some mellow tunes on my Walkman, or grab a little food. Occasionally I chat with other athletes, but mostly I keep to myself. Terry Franson, my coach, stops in to check on me.

Before long we're called out for the long jump. It is mid-morning, and slightly cool since we're in the shadow of the stadium. When my turn comes, I normally get very intense, as if I want to kill somebody, and I get pumped up until the adrenaline flows, and then I burst down the runway. I run faster by imagining that something evil is chasing me and that it's a matter of life or death whether I can beat it out and get off the toeboard. After I land, my distance and my score are announced, and then I immediately try to forget it—completely—because I know I've got to do the same thing two more times. I'm riding a mental roller coaster—getting my adrenaline up, bringing it down, getting it up again, bringing it down. Today, however, I don't feel enough of the intensity. It's only my second event, and I'm struggling to stay focused.

I know I need prayer right now, and I'd jump at the chance to pray with someone down here on the field. But there's no one I know well enough to ask, so I simply jump. My final distance of about 23'4" earns me good points. And my ankle, which was sore before the Games, doesn't bother me.

After the long jump is over, I have to completely relax again and wait for the shot put to begin. The event lasts about an hour, from 1 to 2 P.M. I warm up, sit and wait to be called, take my turn at heaving the sixteen-pound shot, then wait for the other thirty-six guys before taking my second throw, and so on. Though it's my least favorite event, I manage a distance of about 47'8"— solid but not spectacular.

In a typical decathlon, I have to wait for thirty to forty-five minutes between events. At the Olympic Games, however, additional activities such as moving TV cameras and equipment, not to mention other athletic events taking place, can increase the waiting periods significantly and throw off your rhythm. Doing the decathlon at the Olympics is completely different from anywhere else, even than the World Championships or the Goodwill Games. It's like playing in the Super Bowl, only more so. The stadium is packed—at least some of the time—and the whole world is watching you on TV. Everywhere you go, reporters, cameras, and admiring fans swarm about. And you realize you're competing

Dave Johnson

not just for yourself but for your country. Everything is at stake.

The high jump takes forever because it involves a bar that must be repositioned each time. And since we're given three attempts at each height, the event can drag on for hours. Today I open at 6'3" and clear it on my first attempt. I decide to pass on the next height and then jump again at 6'5". Decathletes do this a lot—making sure they clear at least one height, then passing to a more challenging one. I feel great after clearing 6'8", but then miss three times at the next height. Not too many points lost, because my best is 6'10".

It is now after 6 P.M., and the 400-meter run is about to begin. TV networks usually broadcast the last event of the day live, so we must wait for cameras and satellite equipment to be positioned and switched on. I place second in my heat with an okay time of 49.15—but my head still isn't in the race. It feels more like training. But at least I've made it through the first day, which for me is the harder of the two days.

Only slightly relieved after the 400, which ended at around 7:30, I grab my gear to leave for the day. I've been here for more than twelve hours. Outside the stadium, my wife, Sheri, her parents, and my parents are waiting, along with one of my cousins, Jim, and my coaches. We all exchange hugs and chat briefly. It's great to see them and to know they're rooting for me. But I won't be able to spend any time with them tonight; I still have to ice down before bed.

I give Sheri a hug. "I love you, thanks for coming, I'll see you tomorrow," I say. All the while, the day's events are still replaying through my brain.

Between the two days of the decathlon, you have to settle yourself down, body and mind, and prepare for the next day. My whole body's been working hard, but my legs have been working the hardest, so I go to the first-aid room and sit in an ice bath for a few minutes until my muscles get completely cold. Then I get out and freeze while they warm back up. The process is supposed to reduce some of the stiffness the next day. By the time I get back to my room it's 10:30 or so, and I know I need to get some sleep. Since I'm required to check in at the stadium before 7 A.M., I'll need to get up by five or six at the latest.

In order to prepare yourself mentally for Day Two, you have to completely forget about Day One. You have to act like the meet hasn't begun yet and that tomorrow's the first day. You hope you can go back to your room and fall asleep right away. No such luck for me—I'm too wired. The noise in the athletes' village certainly doesn't help. Most of the thousands of other athletes have already finished, and they've been partying every night. Finally I put on some headphones and listen to a relaxing tape with the sound of the ocean surf. It's probably two or three in the morning before I "think" myself to sleep.

Only a few hours later I fall out of bed. My body is stiff and sore. In spite of the ice bath, my legs feel like they've been hit with baseball bats. In other words, I feel completely normal for a decathlete on the morning of his second day.

I look for other decathletes in the huge dining area. How can so many people be up so early? To one side I notice the decathletes from the USSR, who don't look tired at all. I grab a cup of coffee with my breakfast to give my body a little jump-start. As I leave for the shuttle to the stadium, I stop in the bathroom and glance into the mirror. At least I don't look as bad as I feel.

The first event of Day Two is the 110-meter high hurdles, a speed and flexibility event. It's one of the most difficult, most technical events of the decathlon, and the hardest to do when your body's sore and tight. After stretching and warming up, I line up in my lane and take a couple of practice starts to get my adrenaline to kick in. At the gun, I explode from the blocks, take eight strides before extending my right leg and then raising the left to clear the first hurdle. Three steps between each of ten hurdles, and it's over. Again I feel relieved that I've started this second day of the decathlon.

The discus begins shortly, at about 9:15, and I'm in the first group. Waiting for my turn, I sit around, stretching and trying to wake up my body more. I've had so little sleep over the past five days that I'm struggling to energize myself and focus on this event. My emotions, my motor skills, and my senses are beginning to feel like burnt-out spark plugs. I foul twice in the actual competition before throwing a weak distance of around 139 feet, ten feet short of my best.

For some reason the officials call us out late for the pole vault. Then they proceed to give thirty-four vaulters only twenty minutes total to warm up—nowhere near the time we're supposed to get. This ticks off all the decathletes, me included. Again and again they have cut short our warm-up time. In the pole vault—the most technical of the ten events—adequate warm-up is essential so that all of us can practice going over the bar until we feel confident.

Dave Johnson

Otherwise something will go wrong, possibly resulting in serious injury.

When the officials announce that it's time to start the event, the first jumper merely sits down in protest. Nearly half of the athletes didn't even get a practice jump, and it wasn't fair. But after his allotted time of two minutes expires, the referees call it a foul and announce the next jumper's name. At that, the rest of us also sit down. We unanimously decide not to move until the officials give us enough warm-up time. By now the crowd has joined in, screaming and hooting in disapproval, and some of the athletes and officials exchange heated words. After fifteen minutes, an English-speaking official comes down on the field and eventually convinces the Korean officials to give us all the time we need.

The pole vault requires more mental energy than any other event. You have to run, properly plant the fiberglass pole, launch your body into the air with it, and follow through correctly with all the motions in order to clear the bar and land safely. If you do something wrong, you might miss the box with your pole and slam into the pads, miss the pit completely once you're airborne, or even break the pole.

When my turn comes to vault, I grab my

pole and get into position. Immediately I feel distracted by the TV cameras and the huge video scoreboard in the stadium, which looms to my right as I face the bar. When I stand at the top of the runway and lift up my pole, I see a camera zooming right into my eyes, and then, up and beyond it, the giant screen with my giant face. As I run toward the bar, the camera and my video image follow along, creating a feeling of disorientation in my peripheral vision.

I still manage to jump pretty well, maxing out at just over sixteen feet. My teammate Tim Bright, however, steals the show by jumping 18'8"—a world decathlon record. His score propels him into fifth place, within striking distance of a medal.

Besides the intrusive TV cameras, the sheer amount of time it takes to complete the pole vault wears you down—especially the waiting between jumps. Today this one event lasts five and a half hours.

By now darkness is setting in, and the crowd thins considerably. But the quieting stadium improves my concentration as I step up for my favorite and best event, the javelin. Today I place second in my group and fifth overall with a distance of 218 feet. My score moves me into

Dave Johnson

the top ten—too far from a medal but not bad for my first Olympic Games.

At around 9:30 P.M., we gather under the lights for the event we've all been dreading from the very start—the 1500-meter run. It's the hardest one to prepare for mentally. Why? Because you have so much trouble getting excited about it. You wish that the final event would only require a quick burst of energy, like the discus or shot put. That you could handle. Instead, however, you are facing the longest event of the decathlon—the one that requires the most endurance and causes the most pain.

And yet, as my group takes off at the gun, I muster the will to hang on for the next four and a half minutes and keep a steady pace. I lock a couple of phrases from pop songs into my head: "I've been waiting for this moment for all my life." "Behind you a runner is born, Don't look back . . . you'll be there." The songs not only drive me forward but also distract me from the physical pain and the mental anxiety over wanting to perform well and score lots of points. Each lap around the track hurts more than the previous one as the oxygen is being depleted from my body. The third lap is the worst, and the hardest one to stay on pace, but once I reach the last 300 meters I release the final burst of energy I've been saving and push over the finish line in 4:29.62.

I've made it. My final score of 8180 points gives me ninth place. Christian Schenk and Torsten Voss of East Germany win the gold and silver medals, and Dave Steen of Canada edges out Britain's Daley Thompson for the bronze.

After I finish, Sheri, all my family members, and my coaches come down on the track and smother me with congratulatory hugs and kisses. I'm deeply grateful for their support. I no longer care that my body's hurting: I have just completed my first Olympics and placed in the top ten, and I feel exhilarated.

As I smile for pictures, however, I hold back a little, as if to say, "Just wait until the next Olympic Games." It is gratifying to reach one of my life goals, but I still have others I'm aiming for: to be the best decathlete in the world, and to win the Olympic gold medal. I've learned a lot about myself and the Olympics here in Seoul. And I'm fired up about the next four years. I know I'm capable of becoming the world's leading decathlete. I can't wait to get back home and train. Number one score. Number one in the world. The gold medal. That's what I'm setting my sights for.

Dave Johnson

2

Early Training

"Okay, here we go," I announce. "When I count to three, we'll all throw at the same time." It's Halloween night, 1978, and I'm talking to the other members of the West Side Gang, my group of high-school buddies in Missoula, Montana. We're too old to trick-or-treat, and there's nothing else to do, so we get together and stir up some trouble in the neighborhood.

Today we're "recycling" dozens of apples that have fallen from a tree near my house. How do we do it? By shelling passing cars and getting them to chase us.

"All set, guys?" I say at last. A pair of headlights approaches from a distance. The cars travel at thirty-five or forty miles an hour, so we have to get the timing just right. "Ready, on the count of three: One . . . Two . . . THREE!"

We watch in silence for a few seconds as the apples and the car glide toward our estimated point of impact.

Boom. Thunk. Bang. Wump.

"Yeah! Got him!" we yell.

Screech.

"Look out," I warn, still on top of the situation. "He's turning around . . . here he comes . . . Okay, scatter!" We all take off in different directions, laughing as we run. Getting chased is the best part. And as always, we don't get caught.

It still amazes me how those days provided me with early training for the three major components of the decathlon—throwing, running, and jumping. I developed a great arm from throwing things at cars—apples, rocks, snowballs, eggs, even bottles on occasion. My speed came from bolting away when the enraged drivers, or the police, came after me. And I acquired my jumping ability from hurdling ditches and clearing fences as I made my escape. Back then, I barely knew what the Olympics were, and I'd never heard of the decathlon.

Dave Johnson

Mostly I knew how to get in trouble—but I'll get to that later.

*   *   *

I grew up in Missoula, Montana, a small city in the western part of the state, but it probably seemed large to both of my parents, who had moved there in the 1950s from North Dakota. I was number four of five kids. Gary and Cathy came first, then a three-year gap before Barb came along, and another three years before I was born in April 1963. My little sister, Lois, arrived when I was two.

I lived by the slogan "Play Hard" long before Reebok thought of it. Everything I played with as a kid I completely wore out. I went through five tricycles—not the plastic Hot Wheels type but the heavy metal trikes with the hard rubber tires. I'd ride so hard and so often that I wore the rubber right off.

I got average grades in school, though my teachers felt I could do better. "He's got great potential," they'd tell my parents. "He just needs to apply himself more." Later on, my guidance counselors also described me as "not reaching my potential." I wasn't really competitive when it came to grades; I was happy with B's and C's. I preferred to save my competitive energies for sports. I wish I'd given more attention to school-work because later on, when I got into college and actually wanted to learn, I found it difficult to develop good study habits.

With two teenagers and three elementary-school kids to keep track of, Mom couldn't have worked an outside job even if she wanted to. Yet she always seemed available to play games with me or drive me to my various sporting events. She worked the concession stand at my Little League ballgames and even kept score for the team one year. She served as den mother for my Cub Scout troop. I always went to her when I got hurt or had a problem.

In contrast, I hardly ever saw my dad—at least before I turned ten—because he worked almost all the time. He operated a log-peeling lathe for Evans Products, a plywood mill in Missoula—often logging in sixteen-hour days, seven days a week.

I do remember some good times with him, though. During my stint with Cub Scouts, he helped me build a racer for the Pinewood Derby two years in a row; I even took second place one of those years. He built a great playhouse for us kids in the backyard, which I hung out in all the way through high school. Whenever he could, he'd join Mom at my Little League games. I liked looking over from the pitcher's mound and seeing him in the stands; it made me want to play all the better. He'd cheer me on at some of my bowling championships. A few times he took me to work with him, gave me a tour of the mill, and showed me the huge machine he operated. I felt proud of what he did, and it helped me a little to know what his long days were like.

But there were times that I hungered to get to know him better and spend more time with him. Over the years, I think his absence fueled in me a growing sense of anger that would erupt during my teenage years.

I remember fondly the family vacations we took each summer. Mom and Dad would load up the red Chrysler station wagon—and eventually all five of us kids—and drive twelve hours to my grandparents' farm in North Dakota. Since Lois and I fought constantly in the car, they'd purposely drive through the night so we'd sleep at least some of the time.

I enjoyed those vacations because there was always something to do. For two weeks we'd ride horses, go fishing in the "crick," annoy the farm animals, or take out Grandpa's .22 rifle and have target practice using just about anything—bottles, cans, birds, turtles. Sometimes I'd "terminate" a few turtles by sticking firecrackers in their shells. I'd also help with chores occasionally, or watch Dad and Grandpa brand cows.

I was around ten when Dad got promoted to supervisor at the mill. He cut back a little on his hours, and we were able to do more things together. He would take me out on Gary's silver Honda 125 trail bike and show me how to ride. I learned quickly, and hoped I could be a motocross racer someday. I would thoughtlessly zip away for a half hour or forty-five minutes at a time, forgetting that Dad might be worrying about me. But when I returned, he'd be waiting for me in the same spot. I remember feeling loved and cared for in those moments.

*   *   *

My earliest understanding of God came through my parents and through the Catholic church we attended every Sunday. I didn't really understand much of the instruction, but I usually liked going because it was a place to meet friends.

I remember knowing that God created the world, that Jesus was God's Son who died on the cross, and that the Virgin Mary was Jesus' Mom who gave birth to him in a miraculous way. I also knew that the Ten Commandments told me I had to be good. But apart from having to be good, I don't remember grasping the importance of God and Jesus to my life. To me it was just a story. I thought I was the ruler of my world.

*   *   *

My parents encouraged me from an early age to play sports. Practically any sport I tried I picked up immediately. At age six I pitched for the Pee Wee League. But I threw so hard that one of the catchers on the team refused to catch for me—my pitches stung his hand too badly. The coach actually tried to get me to slow down because he was afraid I'd throw out my arm.

After Pee Wee came Little League baseball, which I played every year until seventh grade. I became the starting pitcher for the team sponsored by Western Federal Bank. I could also hit. With each season I tried harder to be the best pitcher, to have the best batting average, or hit the most home runs. But I only pushed myself during the actual games; I didn't think about it much otherwise. I played well, had fun, and made the all-star team each year, but I never really took baseball seriously. To me, baseball was just a game, like Monopoly. You pull out the board, play for awhile, and then put it away.

A similar pattern occurred with bowling, a

sport both of my parents enjoyed. Mom bowled in a morning league when I was three or four, and she'd bring me and Lois along because the alley had babysitting. She and Dad would bowl together on Friday nights. When I turned eight, they let me join a kids' bowling league with my friends Rick and Steve. I liked it, and again it came naturally for me. The three of us bowled on the same team for the next seven years, with one new kid each year. We racked up victory after victory, and I got all kinds of trophies. I was the league high bowler, the league president, and the league team captain. As a seventh grader I bowled a 223 game. Our team was so good that we were moved up to the next higher league with kids two or three years older—and we won there, too. But as with baseball, I didn't think much about bowling once I left the alley.

Besides those two sports, I was always involved in pick-up football and basketball games with friends. I remember high-jumping in the back yard with my oldest sister Cathy, who ran track in high school, and Barb. And we always raced each other everywhere.

Sometime during junior high I lost interest in baseball and bowling—in all organized sports, for that matter—and my behavior took a decidedly negative turn. Why? For one thing, Mom

Dave Johnson

got her first job. She worked afternoons at a local delicatessen from two to seven, which left us kids "home alone" after school. Up to this point, she had done her best to keep me in line, but since Dad worked so much, he wasn't around to enforce the limits she set. Now, with Mom away too, I seized the opportunity for adventure.

Another factor was the onset of my adolescence, and all that went with it—the desire for independence from my parents, the freedom to do whatever I wanted without having to answer to anyone, the need to develop a sense of my own identity. I never had any heroes or role models to help me figure out the kind of person I wanted to be; I never looked up to anyone. All I knew was that I wanted to be *somebody*. So I ended up turning to my friends to meet these needs.

Unfortunately, the things I did with my friends weren't exactly safe and wholesome. Sometimes we'd try something daring just for the thrill. When it snowed, we'd play "hooky-bob," that is, we'd hang on to the back bumpers of moving cars and slide behind them on the slippery roads. We did all kinds of stunts on our bicycles—jumping over ditches, ramps, even each other.

Or we'd experiment with firecrackers. Once,

around the Fourth of July, I stuck a firecracker in a partially filled gasoline can in the driveway. Of course it was stupid, but I wanted to see what would happen. I dashed away just in time to see it blow right into the side of the house with a great *foom*. The explosion really scared me—not to mention the flaming gasoline. Dad came flying out of the house, and with the help of a neighbor hosed down the fire. He grounded me, but I think he was more relieved that I was okay and that I hadn't burned the house down.

Many of our stunts and pranks involved cars: We always tried to get passing cars to stop and chase us. One trick we used was to lie by the side of the road to make it look as though we'd been hit by a car. I'd put ketchup all over my face, and then lie with my head up against a telephone pole, pretending to be unconscious. The other guys would hide in the bushes and watch for cops. Inevitably a car would pull over and someone would come running over to me. I'd stay still until he got pretty close, but then suddenly I'd jump up, scare the daylights out of him, and we'd all take off running.

As we got bolder, we'd get cars to stop by throwing rocks or apples or eggs at them, not caring that we were damaging property. The rush came partly from hitting the cars, but mostly

Dave Johnson

from getting chased. We ran too fast and hid too well for anyone to catch us, even the cops.

The more stunts we pulled, the more cohesive my little band of friends became. We proudly called ourselves the West Side Gang, and we gathered regularly in the playhouse Dad had built, to plot new ways to terrorize the neighborhood. But it wasn't long before our rabble-rousing led to actual law-breaking.

I remember the first time I stole something and got away with it. A couple of my friends and I had gone into McClay's, a corner store near my house. While I was looking at all the candy, I picked up a foot-long stick of bubble gum and played around with it. I noticed I could easily stick it up my sleeve. I intended to buy it, but when I saw my friends leaving the store, I just followed them out, forgetting that I still had the gum up my sleeve. Afterward I realized how easy it was to snitch and not get caught.

Eventually we started to shoplift more regularly—usually candy. One time we got caught, and I figured we were in big trouble, but the manager let us off with a stern warning.

So began my life of petty crime with the West Side Gang. As we entered high school, however, our illegal activities would get much worse.

Dave Johnson

3

Trouble Brewing

During tenth and eleventh grade at Sentinel High School, I again settled for average academic performance, and I didn't play sports. School didn't mean all that much to me. I couldn't wait to meet Mike and Rick and Steve and the other West Side Gang members after school got out each day.

We still loved nailing cars and being chased, but now we had discovered a new pastime: drinking. Alcohol made us feel braver and wilder —even if it did get us into major trouble.

The cheapest and funnest way to get the

stuff was to steal it. By now we'd perfected our shoplifting technique. Sometimes I'd go straight to the beer section of a 7-Eleven, stick a six-pack under my coat, and walk right out. But this approach only worked for small quantities. If we wanted a larger supply, we would have to look elsewhere.

Soon we began to break into places in search of alcohol, or money to buy it. It started with houses, mostly in our neighborhood. Then one night I raided a pizza joint after it had closed, and even used one of their delivery trucks to bring all the loot home. Another time we broke into a bar.

The day after a break-in, I discovered that the good feeling didn't last. The antics that had seemed so fun the night before looked childish and stupid. I'd be afraid of getting caught. And I'd begin to think of the people who lived in the house, and how they must have felt when they saw the damage I'd caused. I actually knew some of these people, and I felt guilty.

By the end of our sophomore year at Sentinel, most of us had gotten our driver's licenses, and we eagerly joined in with the school party scene. We took it upon ourselves to bring beer whenever we could find or steal it.

Dave Johnson

But the demand was high, and our supply was low.

One night during the fall of my junior year, I unexpectedly came upon the opportunity of a lifetime—or so I thought. It was after midnight, and as usual I wanted to prowl, so I snuck out my window and roamed around the neighborhood. I noticed a car parked in front of the Sandman's house with a red Budweiser logo on the door—some kind of company car.

There wasn't any beer in it, but I did see a large ring of keys, perhaps fifteen in all, lying on the seat. The idea occurred to me to start a key collection. I'd keep my eyes open wherever I went, and any time I saw keys I'd take them—just so I could say I did it. I figured this fat ring would make a good starter set, so I grabbed it.

A few days later it hit me that these keys probably went to a Budweiser place. Could it be that I'd actually gained access to an unlimited supply of beer?

First we had to find the place. After checking the phone book and driving around, we located a big warehouse on the other side of town. Then, a few nights later, six or seven of us went back, parked our cars down the street, and strode up to the side door. On it was a large "Beware of Dog" sign. We didn't see any dogs, but just to be sure, we banged on the door and the windows and listened for barking. The noise would probably also trigger a sound or vibration alarm if there was one. We sat in the bushes for a while, and when no dogs or cops appeared, we started trying keys in the door. Sure enough, one of them turned both the deadbolt and the knob lock, and the door clicked open. The magic key.

My heart raced with excitement and fear as we proceeded very slowly with our flashlights into a dark hallway. We were still terrified that a guard dog might suddenly attack us; maybe some dogs were specially trained to kill without barking. And motion sensors could set off an alarm, so that worried us, too. It seemed like a long time before we reached the end of the hall and opened the door into the warehouse.

What an incredible sight.

Aisles and aisles of beer, more than we could drink in a lifetime, stacked to the ceiling. Cases upon cases of every imaginable alcoholic beverage. All ours for the taking.

We hardly knew where to start. The thrill of our discovery quickly dissipated our fear of dogs and alarms, and we began to roam up and down the rows, surveying the supplies and trying to decide what to take. Several lights were appar-

Trouble Brewing

ently left on in the room at all times, enabling us to see without any trouble. Besides the expected Bud and Bud Light, we found other beers, ales, wines, and concoctions we'd never heard of, so of course we had to sample each of those. There was also a keg room, so we lugged out a keg to bring with us. We felt like little kids who'd been set loose in Toys R Us.

After two hours of drinking and discovery in this newly found paradise, we decided to collect our treasure and bring it home. We didn't want to use the same door we had entered by, because the outside area was too well-lit, so we carried everything to the rear loading dock. We found the control box for the huge garage doors, and raised one of them only a few feet, just high enough for us to slip under. Moving quickly now, we carted everything out underneath the garage door and stacked it in a dark corner. Going back inside, we closed the dock door, retraced our steps and cleaned up, making sure the place looked the way we found it. All the bottles and cans we'd drunk from went into the garbage— not really a smart place, since someone could notice them and get suspicious. (They did get suspicious, I later learned, but only of the employees.) Then we left the building through the original entry door and locked it.

Dave Johnson

Finally, one of the guys drove the car around to the back, where we loaded it up in about three minutes and then blew out of there as fast as we could.

"Yeah, we did it!" we yelled in the car. "This is *it*—the best we've ever done!" The whole way home we whooped and gave each other "high fives." We were so jazzed that we'd pulled such a big heist and gotten away with it. Not to mention dead tired from all the hard "work" we'd done.

But this was only the beginning. It wasn't a one-time job like the pizza place; I still had the magic key, so we could go back to this warehouse as often as we liked. The potential seemed enormous.

We returned to the warehouse pretty much every week for the next seven or eight months. I lost track of all the parties we either sponsored or provided alcohol for. Sometimes we'd bring other friends to help us select what we needed for the next week's party, and once or twice we had as many as ten people in the building. It still amazes me that we went for that long without getting caught.

As spring came and the school year began to wind down, the West Side Gang planned to supply kegs for a major party at a friend's house. So on Thursday night we hopped in the car for our usual run to the Bud warehouse. It would turn out to be anything but usual.

When I stuck the key into the door, it wouldn't turn. *There must be something wrong with the lock*, I thought, and kept trying. I pulled it out and shoved it back in several times, wiggled it like crazy, and finally tried to force it in both directions.

Snap.

My magic key had just lost its magic.

Half of it lay in my hand, and the other half remained in the lock. I stood there in disbelief. They must have changed the locks. What lousy timing! Now what would we do?

We didn't even consider backing out of the party. We simply had to have this beer, specifically the kegs. So we went around the building, selected a strategic window to break, unlatched it, and let ourselves in. We spent only fifteen or twenty minutes inside but still rounded up everything we needed—the kegs, a few extra cases of regular beer, and several bottles of wine. Then we split.

What a great party it was, with lots of girls and lots of beer. But I didn't feel good about the situation we'd gotten into. I knew that since we'd actually broken into the warehouse this time, the incident would be reported to the police.

Dave Johnson

Saturday morning I woke up feeling hung over and leery about the previous night. Sure enough, the phone rang and it was Mike. The cops had just shown up at his friend's house and confiscated the kegs we'd left behind. Apparently they'd gotten a lead from someone at the party who knew someone at the Bud warehouse. Mike's friend had given the police two names: Mike's and mine.

Panicking over the phone, we first tried to plot out how we'd protect the rest of the group. But after several long conversations with each other and some of the other guys, we decided we'd all confess together. I'd hardly hung up the phone when there came a knock at the door. I knew who it was, so I let my parents answer.

"Mr. and Mrs. Johnson," the policeman said, "we need to have you and your son come down to the station. We want to question him."

Mom and Dad didn't appear alarmed at first; they'd gotten used to police visits at the house. They just wore the usual disappointed look on their faces as we drove to the station, but once they heard about the extent of my criminal activity, they grew much more concerned. I started crying in front of them and the police, offering up any excuse I could think of. I tried to divert the blame, saying that I didn't cause everything, that the others helped, and that I probably wouldn't have done it if my friends weren't along.

After taking inventory, the owner determined that we had stolen well over five thousand dollars' worth of alcohol. If he decided to press charges, we could be convicted and sent to a juvenile detention facility. We'd have a criminal record. This was the first time I really had to face the law. I'd laughed at it many times, but not now.

After a long conversation between Dad and the owner and the police, the owner agreed not to press charges. Instead, we'd be required to work for the owner until the stolen goods were paid off. We'd have to spend the summer sweeping, chopping weeds, and doing other odd jobs at the warehouse.

My brushes with the law had their effect on me. I began to give myself the same labels that others were using about me: Troublemaker. Bad Kid. The guy who'd never amount to anything. If I didn't make some changes in my life soon, I realized, I'd be headed for an extended stay in prison. The problem was, I didn't know how to change. I didn't really think it was possible to change. So I just figured I was stuck being a bad kid and that there was nothing I could do.

4

Getting on Track

I'd probably be in jail today if it weren't for two big things that happened to me that summer and my senior year of high school. Just as I was headed into more trouble with the law, my dad got transferred to Corvallis, Oregon, and suddenly we had moved away from Missoula. It was hard to leave, but I tried to make the best of my new home and school. I decided to go out for the football team in order to make some friends.

I lied and told the football coach that I was a wide receiver and that I'd played for several years in Montana. Though I didn't know much about plays and patterns, I ran at least as fast as the other wide receivers, and I could catch the ball well. But because the other three receivers had seniority, I had to settle for fourth string. I did become the first-string kick return-er, however.

Since I didn't have any good friends yet, I poured my energy into working harder on the team, showing up for all the practices, sticking with the drills when others were goofing off, and taking extra time to work out in the weight room. Soon I began to make friends and fit into the jock and party crowd. But inside, I felt afraid and insecure.

I got to know three guys during the football season. Terry, a running back, liked to smoke marijuana and go to parties, and he ushered me into the Crescent Valley High social scene. Amit, the place-kicker, was a fun guy to hang around with, and occasionally I could talk to him. My third friend, Matt Hirte, was completely different. He, too, was a wide receiver, and since he was third string and I was fourth, we'd often stand on the sidelines together during games, as well as do the same routines in practice.

My friendship with Matt led to the second major thing that happened to me senior year.

Dave Johnson

What made him different were the things we talked about. He didn't seem to care about the typical jock topics—girls, getting drunk, and pranks. Instead, he'd tell me about his spiritual life, something I'd never heard of, and about Christ, whom I *had* heard of but rarely thought about. To Matt, Christ was not a character in some old fairy tale but a living person you could talk to and learn from and draw strength from. Christ gave purpose and direction to his life, he said, and helped him to live in a positive way.

I thought he was pretty weird at first. People just don't talk about God out of the blue—especially high school kids. But maybe that was the very reason I kept listening. Matt's faith obviously meant a lot to him, and it seemed to help him in his everyday life. The idea of having a *relationship* with God intrigued me. How could you have a relationship with someone you couldn't see—especially someone like God?

Matt belonged to a Christian youth group in the area, and invited me to their basketball night. I had a good time. Before the game, the leader read something out of the Bible, talked about it briefly, and then said a prayer. The other kids seemed eager to learn about God and the Bible. Most of them acted like someone else was the center of the universe rather than themselves—a loving and powerful God who wanted to guide their lives. Curiosity began to grow within me about who Jesus Christ was and whether he had anything to do with me.

Curiosity is one thing; change is quite another. At the same time I was talking about spiritual things with Matt, I was also going out drinking with Terry. The parties we went to always had plenty of beer, wine, and also marijuana, so I began to smoke sometimes, too.

Rather than hide these habits from Matt, I'd ask him to join in.

"C'mon, Matt, we're gonna have a lot of fun tonight—we'll meet some girls."

The first time I asked him, his response caught me off guard.

"Thanks, Dave," he said, "but I don't need to do that. It's just not part of what I want to do with my life."

His honesty struck me. He knew those activities took his life in a direction he didn't want to go. And not only did he know it but he was able to express it around his friends—something I'd never heard anybody do before. He didn't judge me or tell me I was going to hell because I wanted to party. He simply said he didn't want to.

Football season ended, and in early March

track season would be starting. Matt and I kept up our friendship; I genuinely liked being around him. We continued to train together during the off-season, and I still went to youth group with him sometimes. As it turned out, Matt ran hurdles on the track team and encouraged me to join him. I had only dabbled in track back in Missoula, but because of Matt, I decided to give it a shot.

Meanwhile, I was smoking marijuana with Perry and his friends more and more frequently—every weekend for sure, and often during the week too. It got to the point where I was smoking pot more than I was drinking, and I began to feel some unnerving side effects.

On a typical weekend night I'd meet Terry and a couple of his friends, we'd smoke some pot and then go to the parties. Once I got there, however, I felt anxious, insecure, even scared around other people. I felt that people thought I was ugly because of my acne, and that I was a geek because I didn't know how to carry on a conversation. Instead of making me forget my problems, pot caused me to focus on them all the more. Plus I was discovering that people didn't like being around me when I was high.

One Saturday night, after heavy smoking and drinking at a party until three in the morning, Terry and I climbed into the cab of a big four-wheel-drive pickup for a ride home. Two other guys jumped in the back, and Barry, the driver, revved the truck's V-8 engine and immediately squealed the tires for our takeoff. I didn't have a good feeling about this ride home.

Moments later we were doing sixty on a winding forty-mph road that skirted the side of a hill. Barry foolishly decided he wanted to take out mailboxes, so he'd swerve off the road, bowl over a few with the truck's huge grille, and swing back onto the pavement again. But after doing this once or twice, we hit some gravel and skidded sideways.

When I felt the back end slip over the edge of the road and pull us downward, I knew this was serious. Below was a steep slope that leveled off into a field. For some reason I knew that as soon as we hit bottom, the truck would roll. Instinctively I grabbed underneath the dashboard and held on to keep from hitting the roof.

As the truck rolled—six or seven times in all—I remember hearing the shattering of glass and the crashing of metal. The bouncing headlight beams made circles in the night like searchlights.

The next thing I knew I was flying through the air. Somehow I had been ejected from the

Dave Johnson

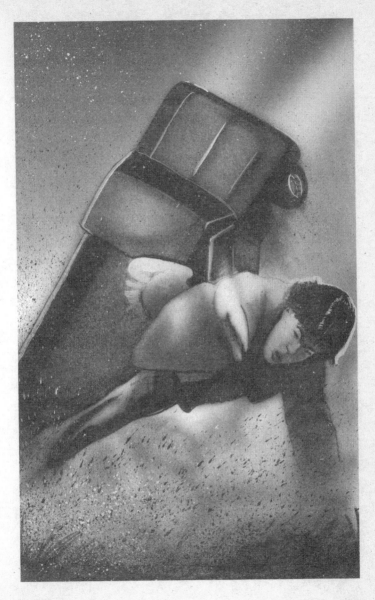

truck, and it seemed like I was floating. But I had a sense of where the ground was, so I simply tucked my head in, landed on my shoulder, took one somersault, and came up on my feet. I had a little scrape on my arm from sliding in the dirt, but nothing else.

I looked over at the truck, which had finally come to rest on its side. The cab where I'd been sitting was crushed completely flat, level with the hood. All was silent.

Suddenly feeling very alert, I called out, "You guys okay?"

One by one we found each other. One of the two guys in back had been thrown clear and only suffered a sore back. The other had torn up his hands badly from gripping the edge of the truck. Terry cracked a vertebra in his neck and had a concussion, but I was able to help him up to the road. That left Barry, the driver. After looking around in the darkness, we found him lying in the bushes forty or fifty feet away from the truck, unconscious. He'd taken a major blow to the head. When the ambulance arrived—a man from a nearby mobile home had called—we were all taken to the hospital.

Exactly how I got out of that truck, especially with no cuts or bruises, I'll never know. I honestly think that God yanked me from that

Dave Johnson

cab and tossed me out of the way. He was protecting me for some reason. And in spite of the others' injuries, it was miraculous that we weren't all killed.

Soon I stopped hanging around with Terry and his buddies. And between the physical danger as well as the emotional torment pot smoking was causing me, I cut way back on the stuff.

After one last bad experience, I simply decided I'd had enough pot. From that point on, when someone asked me to smoke with them, I'd say, "No thanks, I'm not gonna do that anymore." People found it a little strange to see me taking a stand, but I didn't care. It actually felt good to say no to something that had been messing me up so much.

By now track season had begun. I hung out mostly with Matt, Amit, and Jim, another guy on the track team. Though I'd put down the pot, I still kept up the drinking.

In the meantime, we were trying to get in shape for track and practice our events. Matt and I worked on the intermediate and the high hurdles, and I couldn't believe how naturally they came. In about two weeks I was "three-stepping" between the hurdles (most beginners take five), and shortly after that I was beating Matt. I also tried the high jump and joined Jim on the mile relay and picked them up so quickly that I beat most of my teammates.

The season went extremely well, and I had a great time. Our mile-relay team placed second in the district and fourth in the state. And I was the top hurdler and the top high jumper on the team.

My track accomplishments gave a strong boost to my flagging self-esteem. I'd been feeling so inept socially that I wondered whether I could do anything right. To discover—or maybe rediscover—that I was good at something made such a difference. Suddenly, here I was, the best hurdler and high jumper in my school for that year. It caught me completely by surprise; it was too good to be an accident. I wondered if the God I'd been hearing about from Matt and the youth group had anything to do with it.

I'd heard Matt talk about Jesus Christ many times, but I'd never taken the time to find out for myself what it all meant. And the positive experience I was having in track only increased my curiosity. I began to talk to more people and ask more questions about Christ. One guy I approached was Kurt Spence, who attended youth group and also went to Crescent Valley. I hung around the youth center a lot, and paid much closer attention during the Bible studies. I was learning all kinds of things from Scripture, from the group leaders, and from the other kids who seemed to feel so good about who they were and where they were going because Christ was in their lives.

The more time I spent with them, the more I sensed a heaviness in myself that they didn't seem to have. Mostly I felt the weight of my past, the guilt for all the trouble I'd caused my parents, other people, and myself. Guilt for defying and lying to my parents and the police. Guilt for all the alcohol and other things I'd stolen, and the places I'd broken into. I didn't want to carry that weight around with me anymore. I wanted to leave it behind and give my life a fresh start.

I knew these other kids weren't perfect or free from all problems. To the contrary, they often talked about their problems and their wrongdoings; but they saw God as someone who gave them help and forgiveness for those problems. So finally one day I went up to Kurt Spence at the youth center.

"Kurt, I think I'm ready to bring Christ into my life."

We went over to a nearby park and sat down on one of the benches to pray. I thanked God for loving me and for sending Jesus Christ to die on the cross. I asked Jesus to take away my sins and forgive me for hurting others. Finally I asked him to take charge of my life and make me into the person he wanted me to be.

Now I could start over again and rebuild my life on a solid foundation. I felt inspired to make the most of the mind and body God had given me. I wanted to set goals for my life.

My parents seemed a little concerned at first, because I'd never told them anything about my interest in Christ or the Bible before. But soon they both saw that I was beginning to change. I was treating them with more love and respect, and instead of ignoring them or refusing to tell them anything, I tried to share more freely with them what was going on in my life. They also noticed I was beginning to hang out with a different, more positive group of people who didn't get into trouble. That sure made Dad breathe easier.

Senior year of high school: a very up-and-down year in which I felt some of my lowest lows and my highest highs—in more ways than one. But during that year three significant things occurred that set the stage for my future as a decathlete: I began to clean up my life (emphasis on *began*); I excelled for the first time in track; and with the help of two special friends, I found God.

Dave Johnson

5

Raw Potential

I hardly saw Kurt or Matt again after the school year began. I attended Western Oregon State College, but I didn't look for a church or a Christian group on campus to get involved in. I knew that my faith was real and alive somewhere inside of me, but I hadn't yet learned how to develop a day-by-day relationship with Christ.

The only way I could express my faith was through sports. Because I was a Christian, I told myself, I was going to give one hundred percent for the Lord. I was going to work my butt off for the football team. And believe me, I did. I pushed myself harder than all the other freshmen and most of the upperclassmen.

There was one thing that put a damper on the whole season, however: I never played in a varsity game. Not one. Not even one play.

By the end of the season, I felt pretty angry at the coaches and at the whole seniority system. So angry, in fact, that I decided not to return to Western Oregon State. I'd finish out the year and then go somewhere else. I honestly think that if I'd been able to play in just one varsity game, I would have stayed there at WOSC, played football four years, and probably pursued a football career.

But it was not meant to be.

Socially, I hung around mostly with guys from the team. I felt more comfortable around them because they respected me for my athletic ability. At that point sports was the only area of my life in which I felt confident.

Though I never fooled around with marijuana or drugs again, I continued my old habit of drinking and partying. It got me into trouble a few times during the year, though I wasn't stealing or doing anything destructive like before.

As spring came around, I continued working on my track skills. And for the very first time, I tried the decathlon at WOSC. The year before, a coach from a nearby community college, David Bakley, had talked to me and suggested I give it a try. I'd never pole vaulted or thrown a discus or a shot before, and they seemed hard at first. But I thrived on the challenge of learning something new.

Even more, I loved the rush of *improving*. It seemed that each week I did better than the last. In the pole vault, for instance, I started off at nine feet, then a week later cleared ten feet, then in another week I cleared eleven feet. When I first tried the discus, several other guys could throw it farther, but after four or five months I was bettering their distances by ten to fifteen feet. Then there was the javelin: I ended up throwing it more than 200 feet, a freshman school record. It amazed me that I could excel so quickly and so naturally—even more so than in high school track.

My very first decathlon took place in March 1982 at Willamette University in Salem. I scored 6297, not bad for my debut. My parents were there, and they couldn't figure out why I wanted to do the decathlon. I remember standing in awe of the winner, Greg Hanson, who scored in the 6800s.

Throughout the season I felt even more thankful to God for watching over me and giving me this special ability in track. He was providing a way for me to be somebody, first through Jesus and second through the sport of track and field.

My process of becoming a solid Christian was slow and awkward. I wanted to get to know Christ better. I wanted him to affect my whole life. But I didn't yet have Christians around me who could help me grow. And I simply wasn't strong enough to seek them out or to survive on my own. So even as I drank and partied all year (less during track season), I always felt that Christ was still waiting patiently for me to give all of my life to him. He wouldn't give up on me.

After working and saving money the following summer and fall, I decided to go to Linn-Benton Community College for the spring semester. Coach Bakley, who had first told me about the decathlon, clearly cared about me—not merely as an athlete, but as a person.

Right away we got to work on the decathlon. Coach Bakley was an excellent technician; he could pinpoint exactly what I needed to do to improve in each event, especially the pole vault. He was also tough on us in a positive way. He had a special ability to see our potential and help us believe we could reach it. At the same time, he told us we should have fun.

I practiced hard. When practices wound down for the day, I'd keep right on working until I was the last guy on the field.

Coach seemed to be as concerned about

Dave Johnson

the rest of our lives as he did about our athletic lives. He reminded us that sports were great, but that the most important thing was to become a good person. He always encouraged us to stick with our classes, keep our grades up (which I actually did!), and stay healthy.

In the decathlon, he taught me how to deal with failure and success. If I did poorly in one event, he'd tell me to let myself feel bad about it—for two minutes. Then I should ask myself, "Okay, what can I learn from this and how can I improve next time?" Finally I should let it go and focus on the next event. The same was true if I did well: savor it for a few minutes, remind myself of the things I did right, and then put it behind me so I can prepare for what's ahead.

I truly enjoyed being on the team. Not only was I able to work hard, but I had a good time. Often during practices I'd back up my Pontiac to the track, open the trunk to expose a big pair of speakers, and blast my car stereo over the field. I made friends with my teammates and encouraged them in their events.

We had a good season as a team, placing second in the district. I was able to help significantly in the open competition, and I did two decathlons. The first was the same meet in which I'd competed the previous year for

Western Oregon State. Greg Hanson won again, scoring over 7000, but I improved to 6746 and second place, setting a new school record. Coach Bakely's training and technical advice had given me a lot more confidence.

It felt great to be doing well, scoring lots of points for the team, and always improving. The whole season was that way—it got better and better. I also discovered that the variety of events became a confidence builder for me. Whether in practice or in a meet, something good would always happen. If I had a weak performance in the shot put, for example, I could turn around and have a great javelin throw.

Linn-Benton hosted the second decathlon in early May, which was a combined meet—the Oregon community college championship and the NJCAA Region 18 championship. This was the big one, and I was psyched. Two days before the meet we had a very light workout in order to conserve energy. Coach Bakley walked up to me carrying a vaulting pole.

"Hey Dave," he said, "a coach friend of mine found this pole and asked me to check it out. Would you be willing to take a run down the runway, plant it, and see if you can figure out what weight it might be?"

"Sure, no problem," I said.

Dave Johnson

Maybe I ran too fast, or had too much energy built up for the meet, but as soon as I planted that pole it snapped like a pencil into three or four pieces. I took a nasty spill, just barely landing in the pit. Even worse, I fell on my right hand and dislocated two fingers. Coach came running to help me up. I tried to shake it off and tell myself I'd be fine for the meet.

When I got up the morning of the meet, my whole hand was still swollen. Two of my fingers didn't work at all, and the others were sore. I could hardly grip anything. But I was so determined to compete that I wasn't going to let anything get in my way.

I jumped in my car and buzzed over to the campus. It was around 8 A.M., two hours before starting time. I parked at the very end of the lot, overlooking the empty track. For the next hour I sat there in the car with my stereo cranked up, surveying the field, flexing my sore hand, and getting myself pumped for this meet. As the energy began to build inside me, so did the feeling that something big was going to come out of the decathlon.

By the time it was over the next day, I had racked up 7225 points, placing first in the district and second in the region. I was exhilarated. That meet was the place I first believed I had a future in the decathlon. It wasn't just the high score but how quickly I'd reached that score. I'd improved nearly a thousand points in just one year and three decathlons. Coach Bakley had a smile on his face that said, "I knew you could do it, Dave."

Meanwhile, I had to think again about a change in the fall. If I stayed at Linn-Benton, I wouldn't be eligible for track, so I started looking for another school. Now it just so happened that while the big regional meet was going on, Greg Hanson had suggested that I consider a school in California—Azusa Pacific University. Its track team had won the NAIA national championship the year before, and it had a number of good decathletes. He also mentioned it was a Christian school.

At that, my ears perked up. A Christian university? What a great idea. The perfect situation. A school with a championship track team, lots of decathletes as good as me or better, and on top of it, a Christian atmosphere. Coach Bakley hadn't heard of it, but he encouraged me to check it out. So I found the number to Azusa Pacific, called them up and asked for the track coach. His name was Terry Franson.

Our conversation was a little rushed because he said he was busy preparing to go to

Dave Johnson

nationals again. But he seemed genuinely interested in me. When I told him my scores, he was impressed: There were only one or two guys at Azusa who had scored higher than my 7225. I had a good feeling about this place.

I also felt good about the experience I'd had at Linn-Benton. I would miss the friends I'd made on the team. To my surprise, they voted me "Most Inspirational" team member. Most of all, I'd miss Coach Bakley, who had been much more than a coach to me. He'd been my first mentor, someone who believed in me even before I believed in myself.

A week after talking with Coach Franson, a big envelope of information on the school arrived. And the following week I found the results of the NAIA national track and field competition in the newspaper. First place—Azusa Pacific University. I was more impressed by the minute: Not only had this Christian university won the nationals, but one of their athletes had won the decathlon.

I hurried to fill out all the application forms. I had to write about how I became a Christian, and how I'd like to grow in my spiritual life. Even though my faith hadn't completely sunk in yet, I think they got the message that my commitment to Christ was real. In late June I found out

I'd been accepted at Azusa. I was psyched.

Six weeks of summer remained before school. During the days I worked at a fiberglass factory near my dad's plant. From time to time Dad would pop in and we'd have a Coke together. On the weekends, however, I kept up the drinking and partying with friends. I'd been doing it for so long now that I didn't know how to stop—even after it got me into trouble again.

I was with a good friend, Jide, who went to Western Oregon State with me and now attended Oregon State right in Corvallis. On this particular night we had been drinking and hanging out around the Oregon State campus, which was completely closed down for the summer. Just for fun, we decided to climb on top of one of the fifteen-story dormitories and see what it was like on the roof. Pretty nice view, actually, until we spotted the campus security cars coming. We tried to hurry down and run, but they caught us and turned us over to the city police.

We were accused of trying to break in. They fingerprinted us, took our mug shots, even conducted a humiliating strip search. At that I broke down and cried. I couldn't believe they were doing this to us just for goofing off. But there was more: They then proceeded to toss us in jail. Jide and I had to spend the night in a five-by-eight-foot pen with nothing but an open toilet and a bed.

As I sat there in that cell, a million thoughts raced through my head. *I can't believe this is happening. I'm a Christian who's going to a Christian university in a couple of weeks, and here I am sitting in jail! What if the school finds out and decides not to let me in? What if I have to stay in jail? What if my parents find out? Why did I do such a stupid thing? I'm supposed to be changing my life now that I'm a Christian.*

Around noon the next day we stood before a judge. He glanced over the paperwork, then looked at us.

"You guys spent the night in jail?" he asked. "For this? You've paid for your crime. You are free to go."

Believe me—we went. Fast. I was so ashamed that I didn't tell Mom and Dad about it until years later.

I can't say that my night in jail brought about a profound change in my life. But maybe Jesus realized I needed this wake-up call from the police in order to start pulling my life together. I felt sorry for flubbing up so badly, and I believed that God forgave me. *I'm gonna be okay,* I told myself afterwards. *I still have a lot of potential to make something of my life.*

6

No Limits

When I arrived at Azusa Pacific University in the fall of 1983, I felt like a blank sheet of paper, one that had been partially crumpled. I had the feeling that my experience at this school would somehow iron out the wrinkles and fill the lines on the paper with valuable insights.

Everything I encountered at APU was new and exciting—my courses, the small classes, the relaxed environment, and the teachers who not only knew their subjects but wanted to be my friend as well. A family atmosphere prevailed. I wanted to learn everything I could.

Dave Johnson

Another new experience was required chapel every Monday, Wednesday, and Friday for an hour. Some students found chapel boring, but because I hadn't gone to church much since I became a Christian, I actually enjoyed it. I liked being able to focus on God, sing songs, and hear teaching from Scripture so often. I felt myself changing and adopting positive values that would make the world a better place.

Meanwhile, Coach Franson called the track team together in October to begin practicing for the indoor season, which runs from December through February. (Outdoor track season goes from March through May.) Three times a week we'd begin practice with a team meeting, where Coach Franson would say a few words and then we'd all pray together. It felt very awkward at first, because I wasn't used to holding someone's hand and praying out loud.

Once I got used to it, however, I found myself looking forward to those meetings. They helped us gain the proper perspective *before* working out. Then, when we began practice, we knew our purpose in being there: to represent Christ on the athletic field. That meant striving to do our absolute best with the abilities he gave us.

Coach Franson was like a father figure to me. He cared about me and the other team members in a special way. He certainly wanted me to be a great athlete, but more than that he wanted me to be a great person, a "warrior for Christ." He stressed that our team was a Christ-centered team, and that we needed to reflect Christ at all times—not only in our performance but in the way we got along with each other, on and off the track. He told us to encourage each other and to resolve our differences quickly or ask his help. As a result, he created a positive and supportive team atmosphere.

My first Azusa decathlon took place in late January. It was an outdoor meet at Cal State-LA, and decathletes from big schools such as UCLA and USC would be there. I was so excited and motivated that I charged onto the track and took first place in collegiate competition and second overall. My score was 7570, nearly 350 points better than my last decathlon at Linn-Benton, and a new school record at APU.

What a great feeling—to get a big score in my first meet as an APU Cougar. Coach Franson was surprised to see such rapid improvement, although he chalked some of it up to the warmer training weather. Even more surprised were the other decathletes on the team. After all, I was the new guy and they'd never seen me compete. That first meet pretty much put their questions to rest.

Dave Johnson

At the same time, however, it raised a new question for me. This was 1984, an Olympic year, and the Games were to be held right here in Los Angeles. The overall winner of the meet had qualified for the Olympic Trials with a score of 7780—only 210 points more than I'd scored. Could I reach the qualifying score of 7625 in time for the Olympic Trials?

I'd never even *thought* about the Olympic Games before; I hardly knew what they were. But after that meet in January it seemed that I kept hearing about the Olympics wherever I went. My curiosity was aroused. I started reading about some of the great decathletes of recent years such as Bruce Jenner and Daley Thompson. And in my workouts I felt like I had so much more energy yet to unleash. The Olympic Games. That's what I wanted to go for. I'd never even seen it on TV before, but I knew I wanted to be there. My main goal for this year, I decided, would be to compete at the Olympic Trials.

A few weeks later, I shared my goal with Coach Franson. Each year he asks everybody on the team to write down his track-and-field goals. I wrote that I wanted to give one hundred percent at all times, and that I wanted my performance—win or lose—to point to Christ's presence in my life. I put down distances, times, and heights that I wanted to reach for each event. Then I added two more items: I wanted to go to the Olympic Trials, and I wanted to score 8000 points.

Coach sat down with me in his office a few days later. He was holding my goal sheet in his hand.

"Dave, we need to talk about this 8000," he said. "You need to be careful—8000 points is a big jump from your present PR (personal record)." He wasn't trying to talk me out of my goal. Instead, like any good coach, he was gently suggesting that I might be trying to achieve more than I was capable of in my first year at APU. He wanted us to set high goals, but he also wanted to prepare us for not reaching them, just in case.

"But Coach, I think I can do it, I really do," I said. "I'll be able to score enough to go to the Trials, and then at the Trials I think I can score 8000 points."

I know he wanted to believe me, but it's still a big leap from 7570 to 8000. His face remained somewhat skeptical.

I knew I couldn't do it on my own. And even with help, it wouldn't be easy. I'd definitely need Coach Franson's expertise and support—which

Dave Johnson

I was already getting. But even more than that, I'd need Jesus Christ to help me.

"Well, okay," Coach said, remaining cautious. "It's good to have that high a goal, but just be prepared in case you don't make it. I'll do everything I can to help."

Training continued into the spring track season. Even in January and February the temperatures were moderate enough for us to practice outdoors. In each event, I felt myself getting stronger. I was pleased with my 7570 in that first decathlon, but I knew I was capable of doing much better. Good things were going to happen; I could feel it.

My next decathlon took place in March at Occidental College in Eagle Rock. I was hoping to do well here and qualify for the Trials, but a few minor things went wrong and threw off my concentration. I scored 7546—a respectable score but disappointing to me because it was the first decathlon in which I hadn't improved over the previous one. It felt like a setback.

Coach Franson helped me sort through my feelings. He reminded me that no one expected me to be the "perfect" decathlete who always scored more points than the last time. Maybe I needed to relax a little, accept that I'm a fallible human being, and try to learn from whatever mistakes I'd made. He didn't tell me to abandon my goals—just to remember that I wouldn't necessarily reach them immediately.

There were two significant meets in April, both in the same week. First was the California Invitational, sponsored by Azusa Pacific. The second, known as the Mt. SAC Relays, was held at Mt. San Antonio College, and was Southern California's biggest track meet. I hadn't yet reached the qualifying score of 7700 to compete in the Mt. SAC relays. So I remained content to do APU's California Invitational Decathlon.

I was more relaxed than usual for the meet, probably because I'd listened to Coach's advice and taken some of the pressure off myself. I realized I didn't need to be Superman. I could just go out there, give it my very best, and trust God with the results.

On the first day I set PRs in three events— 100, long jump, and high jump—and a PR for my first day total. The second day went even better, with PRs in the hurdles, pole vault, and javelin. My final score? 8043 points. Barely two months after writing down my goals, I'd suddenly reached both of them in one fell swoop. I'd qualified for the Olympic Trials, and I'd passed the 8000 mark.

The high score blew me away. A typical

Dave Johnson

decathlete might score 5900 or 6000 in his first meet. By his tenth decathlon, he may be in the 7500 to 7800 range. This was only the sixth decathlon of my life, and I'd scored over 8000. News of the meet hit the sports page the next day. This twenty-year-old kid no one had ever heard of had just qualified for the Olympic Trials, and his score was high enough to make him a serious contender for the Olympic team. At that time, the top decathlete in the United States had scored 8200 points, and the second-best score was around 8100. I was amazed to discover I had come that close to the best in the country.

That incredible week still hadn't ended yet. A day later I ran the shuttle hurdles for APU at the Mt. SAC Relays. In the shuttle hurdles, a team runs the 110-meter hurdles four times, one runner for each stretch. Energized by my decathlon performance, I took off and ran a 13.9 split—my best ever—and we won first place. Afterwards, the other coaches were coming up to Franson and saying, "Who is this Dave Johnson guy? He scores over 8000 yesterday in the decathlon, and then today he runs a 13.9 hurdles!"

Coach Franson was one proud papa. My respect and trust in him grew because he had drawn me closer to Christ, the One who inspired

Dave Johnson

me to excel. He had also supported me in reaching my goals in spite of his doubts. I began to think that with Christ at the center of my life, there might be no limit to what I could achieve.

The Olympic Trials were to take place in June. But first we had the NAIA nationals in Charleston, West Virginia in May. Coach and I decided to pass on the decathlon at the nationals in order to save myself for the Trials. I'd throw the javelin, do the hurdles, and run the mile relay. Looking back, that might have been a mistake.

For the second year in a row, APU won the NAIA national championships. I took second place in the javelin with a throw of 239 feet. My other two events didn't go as well: I tripped over a hurdle and didn't make it to the finals in that event, and our mile relay team was disqualified because one of the guys stepped on the lane line. But it still felt great to win the nationals.

Only a few weeks later, I had to face a major disappointment at the Olympic Trials, held in the Los Angeles Coliseum. Even after much preparation and training, I only managed a score of 7670, good for eleventh place out of fifty-four decathletes. I didn't bomb in any of the events, but I didn't outdo myself, either. This had been the biggest meet of my life—the first with a large crowd, major media coverage, and twice as many decathletes as I'd ever seen in one place. At the time I couldn't figure out what my problem was. I knew I was capable of winning a spot on the Olympic team, and I'd been trusting God for strength. What had happened?

Looking back, I'd say it was a matter of too much, too soon. This was only my seventh decathlon ever, and my very first at the national level. I hadn't had enough experience yet to feel relaxed and compete effectively in a big meet. Up to that point, my biggest meet had been the NAIA nationals a few weeks back, and I hadn't done the decathlon there. Perhaps if I had, I would have been a little better prepared, but probably not by much.

In one short year, I had gone from a small meet at an Oregon community college to one of the largest and most important meets in the country. From competing before a handful of family members to facing thousands of spectators in the Coliseum. I didn't know how to handle the pressure yet.

I needed more time. More experience. As I prepared for the coming school year, I vowed to begin training hard for 1988.

7

Quest for the Best

My first year at Azusa Pacific University had been a time of incredible growth and discovery. In only nine short months, that school had affected virtually every area of my life. Well, every area except one: my love life.

But in the fall of 1984, even that changed when I met Sheri Jordan, a nursing student from the town of Sweet Home, Oregon, just forty-five minutes from Corvallis. The more time I spent with her, the more things I liked. I admired her strong Christian faith and the seriousness with which she took her studies at APU. She had lots of energy, worked hard at whatever she did and had set high goals for her nursing career. And on top of it, she was one beautiful woman. We would continue dating for several years. After all, she was only a freshman, and I was a junior still trying to figure out my life.

After three straight years of dramatic improvement in the decathlon, in 1985 I finally had what I'd call an average year. I did four decathlons but never passed the 8000 mark—although I got close once or twice. I felt like I was improving in my events, but I just wasn't getting the additional points. At the Fresno State Decathlon in April, I took first place with a score of 7948.

Then in May we went to the NAIA nationals in Hillsdale, Michigan. This time I would do the decathlon there, and I was favored to win. My first day went very well; I was leading the pack at the end of the day, and I had PR'd in the long jump and shot put, and come close to my PRs in the other events. If I continued at this pace, I'd probably break the NAIA nationals record by 500 points. This would be the big victory, the big breakthrough I needed.

On the second day I got good points in the hurdles and discus. But then something went wrong with the pole vault. It was one of my

Dave Johnson

weaker events at this point, and I hadn't trained for it well enough during the year. Still, I figured I'd have no trouble clearing my opening height of twelve feet. Unfortunately, I couldn't get my approach down, and I bailed out of my first jump. My second and third attempts were even worse.

I was crushed. Here I was, the odds-on favorite to win the nationals, and I had just no-heighted in the pole vault. My score for that event, zero, made it virtually impossible to win. I felt so sad and upset that I just wanted to quit the meet. But Coach Franson urged me to finish out the last two events, the javelin and the 1500 meters.

My final score was only 7255, a pretty unimpressive total.

"Hey, it's okay," Coach told me afterward. "Remember, 7255 may be an ordinary score for *ten* events, but it's an excellent score for *nine* events." His words brought some comfort but not the championship.

My next meet was the National TAC Championships in Indianapolis, equal to the Olympic Trials in significance. Most of the best decathletes in the country were there. I turned in a better performance this time, placing fourth with a score of 7911. I struggled again with the pole vault but at least managed to clear one height—13'1". The score gave me my first national ranking: fifth in the United States.

I had one more unfortunate experience with the pole vault at the Olympic Festival meet in Baton Rouge, Louisiana. My vaulting confidence was at an all-time low, and I no-heighted once again. This time I placed fifth out of six decathletes. But afterward I resolved not to let this disaster happen again. Coach and I worked very hard on my vaulting skills, and I would later get some extra help from Coach Bakley.

My national ranking qualified me for a very special honor that summer, however: a week-long decathlon camp at the Olympic Training Center in Colorado Springs. When I heard I was going, I ran to the phone to call my parents. They were as excited as I was.

The program brought together the country's top decathletes for a week of specialized training. We worked with scientists, doctors, psychologists, and other experts on every aspect of the decathlon. I learned all kinds of things about the way my muscles and bones work—not to mention my mind—while I'm in the midst of competition. I also had a lot of fun getting to know the other athletes. But most of all I felt the exhilaration of just being there at the Olympic

Training Center, the place where Olympians were made. One day I'd be one of those Olympians, I told myself.

That week gave me a major boost. I needed it badly at that point because I was now on my own and I felt like I had nowhere to go. My track eligibility and my scholarship money had both expired. Coach Franson had assured me that I could still train with the team, but I knew it wouldn't be the same.

It certainly wasn't. In fact, the entire 1985–86 school year turned out to be very difficult for me. Nothing seemed to go right. I had trouble scraping enough money together to pay my tuition and then did so poorly in my classes that I ended up dropping them all. And since I couldn't officially compete with the Azusa team—I could only compete as an individual—I felt pretty demoralized.

It showed in my first two decathlons of 1986. I could only muster a score of 7791 at the Fresno State Decathlon in March, and a 7635 at the California Invitational in April. The second was the same meet in which I'd scored 8043 two years before.

What a major disappointment. *Man,* I wondered, *maybe the Lord's telling me my time's up*

*for the decathlon. Maybe I just need to quit train-
ing, get a job and finish school.*

But then something stopped me from
believing those words—a feeling from within that
I think came from the Lord. *Don't give up yet,
Dave,* was the message. *It's going to be okay.
Don't be afraid of being alone, of not being on
the track team. Give it another try—not a half
effort but your very best effort.*

I decided to trust God and give myself one
more chance. The U.S. Championships were
coming up in June. For the next two months, I
would train harder than I'd ever trained in my
life, and then go for broke in that meet. If I didn't
do well, I'd accept it as an indication from God
that it was time to quit the decathlon and move
on with my life.

I worked my butt off those two months up
on Azusa's hillside campus, which was empty
because it was being sold. First thing every
morning, high above the L.A. rat race, I'd sprint
up and down the fire road again and again. It was
a time to be alone with myself and with God. I
grew much more focused, much more confident,
and much less afraid. Mostly I think I grew up.

The TAC National Championships were
held in Eugene, Oregon on June 18–19. My parents came, and so did Sheri's parents, who had

Dave Johnson

never seen me compete before. After all my training on the hill, I felt so ready for this meet. I wasn't going to let anything distract me.

I felt strong in almost every event, finishing the first day in the lead with a better-than-average score of 4133. I PR'd in the long jump by nine inches, and two events later PR'd in the high jump. One moment I'll never forget occurred during the high jump, when the bar was raised to 6'9"—a height I'd never cleared. As I stood there preparing to make my approach, the announcer's voice came over the PA: "If Dave Johnson makes this jump, he will literally leap into the lead." His comment got me so fired up that I cleared it on my first attempt.

Once I had the lead, I never lost it. On the second day, another PR in the discus (151'5") gave me additional insurance, and I won the meet with a total score of 8203, my highest ever.

I could hardly contain my excitement. Barely two months ago I'd almost given up the decathlon for good. Now, suddenly, I was the U.S. champion.

That victory was one of the biggest turning points in my career—in my life. God had answered all my doubts, all my questions, all my fears, with a clear message: *Yes, I'm with you and I'm taking care of you. Yes, the decathlon is part of your future. Yes, you can be confident in pursuing it as long as you put me first.*

Up to this point I had just wanted to be good at the decathlon. But now I no longer wanted simply to be good—I wanted to be the best. After all, would Christ want me to strive for anything less? If *he* were a decathlete, there'd be no scoring tables high enough to accommodate him. And since my calling is to be as much like Christ as I can, I shouldn't place any limits on what I could score, either.

The confidence I'd gained through my hill training and my victory in Eugene also spurred me to take the next step in my relationship with Sheri. Our two-year dating relationship had grown into love, and now I knew I was ready to ask for her hand in marriage. I didn't know *exactly* how everything would work out, but I felt secure enough in the direction God was pointing. As national decathlon champion, I figured I'd be able to earn enough money from sponsors to support my wife and me. So a few weeks after winning the U.S. championship I asked Sheri to marry me.

"Really?" she said, smiling. "You're not joking?"

"No, I mean it," I said, smiling back. "I'm not kidding."

"Okay," she said, "if you're really serious, write it down on paper." So I grabbed a pen and wrote, "Sheri, I really do want to marry you. You are the one for me. Please take my hand in marriage forever." She looked at the paper for a second, then threw her arms around me.

"Yes!" she said.

My confidence now soared—all the way to Houston and the Olympic Festival. It's called the Olympic Festival because it's designed to give athletes the experience of being in a big meet. This was the same meet I'd no-heighted in the year before. In the sweltering heat (over 100 degrees), I took first place with a score of 8123.

In September I flew to Talence, France, for my first international meet. I'd never traveled outside of North America before, and I was psyched—not only because of the new opportunity, but also because Coach Franson was coming along.

I charged into the meet with a good time in the 100 meters. However, in only the second event, the long jump, I had a problem. In my excitement, I ran a little too aggressively and fouled my first two jumps.

For my last attempt I tried to settle down and back my step up, but as soon as my foot pounded the board and sent me into the air, I thought for sure I'd gone over the line. *Oh man, I fouled*, I thought. Apparently the crowd thought so too, because I heard them groan, "Ohhhhhh." Assuming I'd fouled, I just stepped down on one foot and ran out of the jump. I had just blown the entire meet.

But then I heard Coach Franson shouting at me. "Dave, what are you *doing*?" he yelled in exasperation. "That was a legal jump!"

It was? Sure enough, the officials had made no foul call. They simply measured from the spot where my one foot had landed. The distance, 20'3", was nearly four feet short of my best at that time. I got 600 points instead of zero, but I *could* have gotten 900 points.

Despairing over my mistake, I immediately wanted to quit. *Why go through the pain of this decathlon when I know I'm not gonna win,* I thought. *I'm not gonna come even close to winning because I lost so many points.*

Coach Franson, ever the encourager, sat me down. "Dave, don't give up yet, it's way too early," he said. "You've gotta trust me on this one. You know in the decathlon anything can happen—somebody else could drop out or blow an event. Stick with it, and you might still be okay. Who knows? You might even win."

I finished out the day with respectable

Dave Johnson

scores. On the second day, I ran a fast hurdles, one of my better times. Then, after throwing a strong discus, it suddenly occurred to me: *Wait a minute—I'm catching up with these guys.* Some of the leaders were faltering, just as Coach had said, and I was getting stronger. A PR in the pole vault brought me up to eighth or ninth in the standings. And a great throw in the javelin landed me in fourth. Finally I ran a solid 1500 meters and ended up in third place, with a score of 7841. In my first international meet, I'd won a bronze medal. And the winner, Christian Plaziat of France, had scored only 100 points more than I had. If I had stayed focused and completed that last long jump, I could have won the whole meet.

*   *   *

Back in Azusa after a whirlwind summer, I resumed my training, this time with the APU team on their beautiful new track. One of my training friends was Kevin Reid, an Azusa student who ran hurdles. He would later become a special friend and play a key role in my decathlon career. By this time I'd moved into an apartment near campus with my friend, Nate. Sheri, now a junior, would stop over and we began making wedding plans. It was great to spend time with her again after an entire summer apart. We settled on a date of June 12, 1987. I was a little nervous that only eleven days later I'd be defending my U.S. decathlon title at the national championships, but I figured everything would work out. The meet would be sort of a honeymoon for us.

To support myself, I had a part-time security job and mowed lawns for a gardening service. I'd been able to scrape by on my own, but now that I would soon be supporting Sheri as well, I needed a reasonable income that would still make it possible for me to train. The U.S. Olympic Committee was sending me some money each month, which helped, but it still wasn't enough for a married couple to live on in Southern California.

So I began writing letters to all kinds of companies that I thought would be interested in sponsoring me. I got a few responses but nothing that really amounted to much in the way of financial help. Then one day I got a call from the president of Blublocker sunglasses. He wanted to fly to California to meet me and talk about the possibility of doing a commercial.

Whoa, I thought, *a commercial? This is too cool.* Sure enough, they decided to include me in a half-hour "infomercial" in which I pole vaulted, ran hurdles, and talked about Blublocker sun-

Dave Johnson

glasses. In exchange, they'd send me $1,000 a month straight through the '88 Olympic Games—and of course, all the Blublockers I needed.

I thought it was a phenomenal deal. God was assuring me that my life was on the right "track." It made me believe he wanted me to be the best. It motivated me to work harder.

To keep myself in top form for the U.S. championships, I competed in Azusa's California Invitational Decathlon in early April. My training had been going so well that I cruised right through the meet and easily won with a score of 8045. Now I could be even more confident for the June TAC nationals in San Jose.

*   *   *

It's difficult to get injured in track and field, but not impossible.

I found that out during a practice in early May. I'd been working on the shot put with Coach Franson and the team. I had just taken a throw, and I stepped out of the ring as usual. Unfortunately, I didn't notice that another shot had rolled up alongside the ring, and I stepped on it, twisting my right ankle. It hurt a little, but no big deal, I thought. I decided to give it a rest for the day.

The next day I resumed training. My ankle

was slightly swollen and a little sore, but I went ahead and ran my workouts anyway. For the next week and a half, the soreness lingered. Then the pain began to increase, a little each day, then a little more, until it really started bothering me. The doctors X-rayed it and concluded that I had a bone spur—a tiny splinter of bone that can aggravate nerve endings and cause a great deal of pain. They told me it would probably go away on its own.

It didn't. In fact, it grew worse. By the first week of June, I was limping so badly that I had to stop working out altogether.

Here I was, one week away from getting married and three weeks away from the U.S. championships. I was looking forward to the wedding and the beginning of married life with Sheri, but I also felt preoccupied with my foot.

We had a beautiful and fun wedding at Sweet Home Mennonite Church in Sweet Home, Oregon. Sheri looked absolutely stunning coming down the aisle. But as I stood next to her, facing the minister, I couldn't help but feel the nagging pain in my ankle. I tried to put it out of my mind and enjoy the occasion.

As if to add insult to my injury, I got a violent case of the flu during our honeymoon, which left the rest of my body very weak. Down in San

Jose at the TAC nationals, I limped through the first day with a very subpar score. On the second day, the sore ankle and the lingering weakness took their toll. I stumbled during the hurdles and placed dead last, then followed up with a mediocre discus throw. I was hurting too much to go any further. For the first time in my career I had to drop out of a meet.

Afterward I felt disappointed but not depressed. It wasn't my fault, I reasoned, it was the bone spur. Before long it would go away and I'd be fine.

Soon after our wedding I learned that I would be getting work through the Olympic Job Opportunity Program. It gave me a half-time job with a company for which I'd receive a full-time salary. That way I'd still be able to train each day. Sheri and I were amazed at how the Lord was providing for us. When I heard who the company was, I couldn't help but laugh: Anheuser-Busch—as in Budweiser, the company I'd stolen all the beer from in Missoula. My duties would involve simple office tasks such as filing or answering phones, and occasional public-relations activities.

In August I traveled with Coach Franson to Saskatoon, Saskatchewan, for a low-key competition. I had thought my foot would be better by now, but it killed me for the entire meet. Don't ask me how I did this, but somehow I just gutted it out and endured the pain. With all the Lord had been doing for me, I really wanted to give him everything I had in this competition. When it was all over, I'd won the whole meet with a score of 7824, which gave me a ranking of eighth in the U.S.

It felt good to win, but I knew something was still wrong with my foot. So I decided to go ahead with surgery to remove the bone spur. The operation took place in October, and the doctors felt that the procedure had been a success. Sheri took time out of her studies to help me through my recovery, which lasted about a month. We were such good friends, and I felt like we were now a team, working together to serve God. In spite of being incapacitated for a time, I felt optimistic that my foot would heal soon and everything would be fine.

8

No Biz Like Shoe Biz

After my ankle surgery in October 1987, I did not compete in any decathlons until the U.S. Olympic Trials in Indianapolis, Indiana, the following July. I trained the best I could, but I still felt too much pain in my ankle to get into the kind of shape I needed to be. As the spring months of 1988 passed, I began to worry that I wouldn't be able to compete in the Trials at all.

What neither I nor the doctors knew during that time was that the problem with my ankle had not been a bone spur. I'd actually broken a bone in my ankle. Either I'd fractured it the moment I stepped on that shot, or possibly I'd knocked it out of adjustment and then fractured it afterward. This type of injury is known as a stress fracture, and it often doesn't show up on standard X-rays.

I know that now. I didn't know it then. Neither did I know how dramatically the injury would alter the course of my career.

About a month before the Trials, the pain suddenly stopped—almost completely. I couldn't understand it, but I sure was thankful. Maybe the Lord wanted me to learn a lesson in trust when I went to the Trials. I spent that last month training as hard as I could.

The day finally arrived—July 20, 1988. When I got up that morning in Indianapolis, I looked out my hotel window and saw rain—not a drizzle, not a shower, but a downpour. It's always a bummer to do some of the events, especially the shot put and high jump, in the rain.

I was nervous. It's scary enough to be facing the meet of your life—where you have to perform at your very best just to make the team, not to mention standing before the largest crowd a decathlete will ever see outside of the Olympic Games itself. But then I had the added factor of utterly miserable weather. It would be much easier to slip, foul, fall, or suffer injury.

As I stepped into the blocks in the drenching rain, I prayed, *Lord, help me to give 100 percent. Please allow me to make this Olympic team.*

I turned in a decent but not spectacular time of 11.14. My ankle, which had been heavily taped, held up well. Since the tape got soaked, however, it had to be removed after each event and replaced with dry tape.

One young athlete raised eyebrows by running 10.83, only a hundredth of a second out of first. His name was Dan O'Brien, someone I'd never heard of before. He would do only one more event before dropping out with an injury.

Next we waded up to the long jump area. Again I was pleasantly surprised by my performance—third best with a distance of 24'1".

Then came the shot put. What a joke. The throwing circle had become a kiddie pool, and even after great vacuums were used to suck out the water, the athletes slipped and fouled through the event. Once we were able to get off a throw, the shot often sank completely into the mud, requiring officials to dig it out with a shovel. I still managed a good throw.

I continued with solid performances in the last two events. By the end of the first water-

Dave Johnson

logged day, Gary Kinder, Tim Bright, and I were in the top three positions.

And that's where we stayed, straight through the second day, which thankfully was sunny and warm. After a great javelin throw and a PR in the 1500, I finished the Trials in third place with a score of 8245, fewer than fifty points out of first. I'd made the team.

What an incredible feeling. Finally I'd made it to the big time. I was going to the Olympic Games to compete against the best in the world.

I'll never forget the exhilaration of running our victory lap, American flag in hand, and waving to the packed stadium of 10,000. When I got around to where Sheri was sitting, she came down from the stands and gave me a big hug and a kiss. It felt so good to show her that some of the dreams I'd been telling her about could actually come true. That experience ranks as one of my life's most special moments. And Sheri admits that from that day on she became hooked on the decathlon.

My parents were so happy for me. Five or six years ago, they wouldn't have dreamed they'd see me in anything but trouble. Now, here I was, about to take off for the Olympic Games.

Only a few weeks passed before Coach Franson and I packed up for Seoul. First we went with the entire U.S. Olympic team to a two-week training camp in Chiba, Japan. I loved the chance to work out alongside the cream of America's athletes and their coaches. My foot seemed pretty strong, though I continued taping it for good measure. I was very psyched for Seoul. I actually believed I could win. I knew I was capable of doing it.

Of course, being *capable* of doing it and actually doing it are two different things. I would learn that the hard way in Seoul, as I describe in the first chapter. There were other factors I hadn't yet learned to account for—the huge crowds, the TV cameras in your face, the burden of representing your country, the much larger field of decathletes, and the much longer waits between events. I felt some of that pressure during the Trials, but during the actual Games the pressure was ten times as great.

Some athletes can easily block out all these distractions, or else use them to their advantage. I was still learning how to stay focused. In fact, my entire time in Seoul was a great learning experience.

As I sat on the plane back to California, I felt relieved and happy. My first four-year Olympic cycle was over. And though I hadn't won, I'd done well and I'd picked up many valuable lessons for next time. I knew I'd be back.

*   *   *

Back at home, Sheri and I resumed our "normal" life. We'd been married for nearly a year and a half, and she was working as an intensive care nurse for infants. I continued training for my first big meet after the Olympics—the TAC Senior Championships on June 13–14, 1989.

The competition took place in Houston, Texas, on two incredibly hot and humid evenings with over-90-degree temperatures. I felt good and PR'd in the first two events, with a 10.79 100 meters and nearly 25 feet in the long jump. With each event that followed, I consistently logged in solid scores, and by the end of the first day I was in second place—a good position since my second day is stronger than that of most decathletes. I felt like I was having a great meet and that I'd probably win.

I didn't realize just how good a meet until late in the second day. Coach Franson had been checking the scoring tables and punching numbers into a calculator. After I ran a pretty fast hurdles, he had determined that I was actually on a pace to break Bruce Jenner's American record of 8634, scored at the 1976 Olympics. Coach didn't say anything to me at first; he didn't want to add any pressure.

Then I PR'd in the pole vault, clearing 16'10". I didn't know it, but with two events remaining, I was now *ahead* of pace for the American record.

"Doing great, Dave," Coach said, maintaining his cool. "Keep it up!"

But Coach's roommate for the meet, decathlon expert Frank Zarnowski, ran to the phone to call his friend Bruce Jenner. There was no answer, but Frank left a message on his machine: "I'm at the TAC meet in Houston. If Dave Johnson throws a good javelin and runs 4:20 in the 1500 meters, he'll be the new American record holder."

Of course I still didn't know what was going on, so I just stepped out to take my javelin throws. After two decent but not spectacular attempts, Coach decided to talk to me.

"Dave, I don't usually do this," he said, "but I think you need to know that you're *very* close to breaking the American record. You need a javelin throw of about 228 feet to have a decent shot at it."

I was stunned, and needed a few seconds to catch my breath. Tears even welled up in my eyes as I realized that my dream of being one of the best was really coming true.

My final throw, however, was only 221 feet. And I ran 4:31 in the 1500, good, but not enough to beat Jenner's score. His record would stand, at least for the time being. Even so, I ended up improving my PR by 300 points with a score of 8549.

I had not only won the meet and the U.S. championship, but I'd just posted the Number One score in the world. It blew me away to realize that if I had posted that score nine months earlier at the Olympic Games, I would have won. Coach Franson and I just looked at each other in amazement and gratitude. We knew that the Lord had brought us together for a very special reason. When I called Sheri that night and told her my score, she was so happy for me that she cried.

As it turned out, I had actually come a lot closer to Bruce Jenner's record than people realized at first. Jenner's 8634 score had been with the old javelin. The new javelin, introduced in 1986, was designed to drop more quickly, resulting in shorter distances. Franson and Zarnowski calculated that if I'd thrown the old javelin, my score would be about 90 points higher, which would have equaled and possibly bettered Jenner's 8634. They both wrote letters explaining the situation to the records committee of The Athletics Congress.

My win in Houston qualified me to attend the World University Games in Duisberg, West Germany, followed by the annual meet in Talence, France. I had about seven weeks to train and prepare.

The World University Games were rainy and cold, but they did give me my first international win with a score of 8216. I enjoyed making friends from the other countries, especially Michael Medved of the Soviet Union. After the meet, the German Federation honored me with an invitation to put my footprint in cement alongside that of great German athletes such as Jürgen Hingsen.

The meet in Talence was the same one I'd done in 1986. It was fun to see some of the athletes I'd competed against in Seoul—Christian Plaziat, Daley Thompson, Mike Smith, and others. I was pleased with my performance, even though I placed second behind Christian, 8438 to 8361. It would have been great to beat him, because I would probably have earned a Number One ranking in the world. Instead, he got the win and the ranking. But I was still proud of my score, my second highest ever.

Back in the U.S., I was thrilled to see a press release from The Athletics Congress Records Committee:

Dave Johnson

Move over, Bruce Jenner, you now share the American decathlon record with Dave Johnson. . . . Johnson could have possibly broken Jenner's mark had he been throwing the same type of javelin Jenner had used. . . . The Records Committee felt that since Johnson was so close to the Jenner mark throwing a different javelin, he should also get credit. Thus Jenner will retain his American record with the notation "old javelin" beside it, while Johnson will also have the American record with the notation "new javelin."

It was amazing to be officially recognized for equaling a mark that had been virtually unchallenged for thirteen years.

What a year 1989 had been—U.S. champion, co-American record holder, World University Games champion, top score in the world. What in the world could be next?

*　　*　　*

The decathlon has always been a low-profile sport in the U.S.—way too low, if you ask me. Up to this point, very little was being done to promote or support the sport in America. It rarely received national media coverage other than at the Olympics. Partly as a result, no American had medaled in the Olympic Games since Bruce Jenner's gold in 1976, and no American had been ranked Number One in the world since 1979. In fact, before I earned the Number Two ranking in 1989, only three other Americans had broken into the top ten on the world list during the entire 1980s.

When my 8549 score was declared a co-American record, however, potential decathlon sponsors began to take notice. For the first time in thirteen years, people were saying that the U.S. had an athlete as good as Bruce Jenner.

A major breakthrough occurred in early 1990 when VISA USA, the credit card company, decided to create the VISA Gold Medal Athlete Program just for decathletes. They agreed to sponsor a series of decathlon camps for the leading U.S. Olympic contenders, beginning with a three-day clinic at San Francisco State in April. Finally the sport was beginning to get the attention it deserved. And now I found myself in the position of leading this resurgence.

The first clinic was intense but impressive—even more so than my visits to the Olympic Training Center. In addition to the army of doctors and technicians, many of the top track-and-field coaches from around the country came to assist in the tests and training sessions. Best of all, four of the five living American gold medalists—Bob Mathias, Milt Campbell, Bill Toomey, and Bruce Jenner—joined us to share their experiences and advice.

This was the first time I'd ever met Bruce, and I felt awkward, but he was friendly and we got along well. I never would have thought that I'd be sharing the American decathlon record with him.

Altogether seventeen decathletes attended the clinic, including one guy I'd been hearing more and more about lately: Dan O'Brien. He'd been hampered by injuries on and off since the '88 Trials, but recently he'd been improving significantly. The rumor was that he was fast and had lots of natural ability.

As I watched Dan during the clinic I could see that he truly had exceptional talent. If he stayed healthy, there was no question he'd be a serious Olympic contender. At the end of the camp, we all said good-bye to each other until the U.S. Championships in June.

Dan looked at me before he left and said, "Dave, watch out—I'm coming."

"Yeah, I know you are," I quickly replied, "and I hope you do."

Two months later, he did—at the U.S. championships at Cerritos College in Norwalk, California. I had trained hard and I was ready, but I hadn't planned for this to be the year's "big meet." I was looking ahead to the Goodwill Games in July. From the crack of the opening gun, Dan made it clear that he meant business. He ran the 100 in 10.40, the second-fastest decathlon 100 in history. I was behind him with a 10.78, still a PR for me.

I had an excellent first day, PR'ing in three events—the 100, the shot put, and the high jump. But Dan was having an incredible day. To give you an idea of just how well we were doing, at the end of five events I was *ahead* of the pace that earned me the American record last year. But I was *trailing* Dan by nearly 300 points.

After the hurdles on the second day, Dan's lead had increased to 339 points. I had four events left to make up the difference.

Fortunately, they were my strongest events. In the discus, I gained 50. And in the pole vault, Dan could only manage 14'1", while I cleared 16'4", hacking 208 points off of his lead. Then in the javelin, I heaved about 35 feet farther than Dan and took the lead by 65 points. By the time I finished the 1500, I'd not only won, but I had amassed 8600 points, the second highest score in American history. Dan ended up in second with 8483.

The Dan and Dave rivalry was born. I loved it.

Only a month later we faced each other again at the Goodwill Games, held this year in Seattle. Jointly sponsored by the U.S. and the former Soviet Union, the affair comes closer than any international competition to the feel of the Olympic Games. Many sports are represented in addition to track and field. TV cameras move in. Instead of tens or hundreds of decathlon spectators, there are thousands. And like the Olympics, gold, silver, and bronze medals are awarded.

In many ways the meet proceeded similarly to the last one. Once again, I was nearly 300 points behind Dan after five events. The next day, after seven events I remained more than 300 points out of the lead. I didn't vault nearly as high as I'd hoped, but still managed to reclaim nearly 200 points. My final javelin throw, a PR of 225'3", pulled me within 23 points of first place with one event left.

I needed to run three seconds faster than Dan in order to win. As we lined up, I prayed, *Lord, I'm going to run my very best and leave the rest up to you. I'll be an example for you even if I end up in second.*

For the first two laps, it was anybody's call. Dan, Canadian Mike Smith, Soviet Roman Terechov, and I packed together and stayed out front. Then, on lap three, Dan drifted back just a little, then a little more, and I knew I'd won the gold. My time was 4:26.19, nearly ten seconds ahead of him. Final score: Johnson 8403, O'Brien 8358.

Man—this was the decathlon at its best.

Meanwhile, my new managers, Bob Mendes and Mike Bone, had been quietly approaching companies about sponsoring me. One company in particular, Reebok, seemed to show a special interest in me and in the decathlon. At a meeting with them in late fall of 1990, Reebok's vice president, Chester Wheeler, said to me, "Dave, we believe you are the world's greatest cross-trainer, and we intend to promote you as such. You will be Reebok's Bo Jackson."

Whoa, I thought, *where do I sign?*

It all felt like it was meant to be. VISA's training camps and support made me feel like part of a team. And now Reebok was making me feel like part of a family. Both sponsorships, combined with the support of my wife and my Azusa family, spurred me to train and work even harder as a decathlete. They also gave me further confirmation that God was taking care of me and making it possible to be a role model for him in the sports world.

9

Who is the World's Greatest Athlete?

The ink had barely dried on the Reebok contract when they slated me to do a TV commercial for their new Pump Reebok line of cross-training shoes, and they wanted it to compete directly with the Nike cross-trainers endorsed by Bo Jackson. It was all in good fun.

I felt pretty nervous as we prepared to film the spot. It was only thirty seconds long, but it took six long hours to shoot. My lines went like this:

"Hi, I'm Dave Johnson. For my training for

the 1992 decathlon, I switched to the Pump from Reebok. When I'm pumped up, my feet have support, protection, and a custom fit for leaping, vaulting, spinning, jumping, sprinting, hurdling, racing, running, throwing, and uh, shot putting! Now *I'm* the guy who knows about cross-training. Pump up—[then I toss the Nike shoe]—and air out."

On paper the lines didn't look hard at all, but I was amazed at how many takes it took to get them just right. The director also changed the backgrounds and moved things around dozens of times.

By this time my financial situation had improved dramatically. More sponsors signed on. Sheri and I had been able to buy a house, and it was now getting to the point where she didn't need to work at the hospital anymore. But she loved her job and wanted to continue. I just felt thankful that God was providing for us in such a wonderful way.

Between training, sponsor work, speaking, and a couple of meets, the spring went by quickly. VISA sponsored another camp in early April right at Azusa Pacific University. Coach Franson served as host, and again it really motivated me to work hard and improve my events. Dan was there, too, and from his performances I could see that he would be even tougher to beat this year. He, too, had recently signed up with Reebok, so we would both be "working" for the same company.

At the end of the camp, Dan came up to me and said good-bye again. He had the same look on his face as he did last year when he had told me to watch out. But for some reason, this time he didn't say anything other than "see you later." Maybe he'd decided to let his body and his performance do the talking.

Later in the month, I did my first decathlon wearing a Reebok jersey—the Mt. SAC Relays, hosted by APU. All went quite smoothly and I won easily with a score of 8267. Mt. SAC felt like more of a practice meet for me, mainly because I was looking ahead to the U.S. Championships in New York. Placing in the top three there would qualify me for the World Championships in Tokyo at the end of August. My goal for New York was first to make the World team, and then second to win the meet. I was hoping to peak in Tokyo with a win and possibly a world record.

As the U.S. meet drew closer, my intensity level rose as usual. But perhaps it was a little higher because I knew I'd be facing Dan for the first time this season. I'd beaten him twice last year, but he posed the most serious threat yet to the national title I'd held for two years.

I flew to New York City a few days ahead of time to get settled and check out the meet location—Downing Stadium on Randalls Island, right in the middle of the East River. My friend Kevin Reid, who'd been hired by Coach Franson as an assistant coach, came along to work with me. We stayed at a nice hotel in Times Square and lifted weights at the New York Athletic Club.

We got up early on June 12—my fourth wedding anniversary—for the first day of the meet. At 11 A.M. under sunny skies, the gun went off to start the 100 meters. Dan and I were in the same heat, and he burned up the track in 10.23, the fastest time ever recorded for a decathlon 100. I ran a healthy 10.87, though it seemed slow compared to Dan's time. It looked like we were in for a high-scoring meet.

In the long jump, I managed a decent leap of 24', but Dan sailed more than two feet farther, racking up more than 1000 points for the second straight event. Then I PR'd in the shot put, only to watch Dan outthrow me by three feet for his own PR. Clouds had moved in and drenched us with rain for the high jump, won again by Dan.

By the end of the 400, Dan had set a new world record for first-day score—a whopping

4747. I was in second with 4269, an excellent score but nearly 500 points behind.

It would be almost impossible to catch him this time. On the second day, his lead increased to nearly 750 points by the end of the pole vault. Even after strong PR's in the javelin and the 1500, I was only able to reclaim about 300 of those points. Dan's final score? 8844, only three points short of Daley Thompson's world record. And mine? 8467, which was my third best ever but a lot less than Dan's.

Dan had blown me off the island.

Actually, I'd had a fine, consistent meet. I'd made the world championship team, my primary goal. But I still felt like I'd lost. To me, I hadn't placed second—I'd been beaten. Bad.

I tried to forget about it and focus on my training for the world championships, but I couldn't get the "loss" out of my mind. I knew I needed a sudden and dramatic improvement in my performance if I wanted to outscore Dan in Tokyo, and it wasn't happening. I grew discouraged. As I thought about it, I realized that God had helped me get through tough times before and that I needed to keep trusting him now.

Trusting God wasn't easy, I found, because I soon began having trouble with my left knee. In July I attempted to compete in the Olympic

Festival at UCLA, but I had to drop out after the first event because the knee was bothering me too much.

The doctors said that I had strained a calf attachment area in my knee. It was weird: I had no trouble vaulting, throwing, high jumping, even running the 1500. I only felt pain when I sprinted.

With the World Championships only a month away, my knee was receiving daily ultrasound and acuscope treatments and began to improve. I was able to do some sprinting and hurdling during the first week of August. I needed to have a healthy knee if I was to do well in Tokyo. I hoped that by God's grace it would get better. And if it didn't, I would have to accept that it wasn't my time yet.

Later that month, I bombed in Tokyo.

Or rather, I couldn't get through the meet and had to drop out. My knee had acted up again a few days beforehand, and gave me too much pain to be competitive. From the moment I took off in the 100, I knew my knee wouldn't last, so I simply tried to hang on as long as I could. There was great TV coverage here in the States, and it seemed like the whole world was watching me as I limped around the track in the 400.

Dave Johnson

"Every step was painful, from ankle to knee," I told NBC reporter Todd Christiansen.

But Coach was still proud of me. "Dave, running that 400 was the most courageous thing you've ever done," he said.

Altogether I completed seven events before withdrawing. The big story was Dan's huge win with a score of 8812.

*   *   *

In October I decided to go ahead with surgery on my knee. All the doctor could find was plica, a kind of fatty tissue. Removing it did not appear to take care of the problem, however, because once I was able to return to the track, it continued to hurt just like before. So the doctor tried a series of cortizone shots, which seemed to help a little. I began to worry that my sponsors would lose interest in me because of getting beat twice and then getting injured.

Then a phone call came from Reebok. Sheri and I were invited to Orlando, Florida, for Reebok's annual convention. Dan would be coming, too, and it seemed they wanted to talk to us about something. They put us up in one of the nice Disney hotels, and gave us free passes to Disney World, Sea World, and Universal Studios. Other than a few appearances at the convention, Sheri and I were able to relax and enjoy ourselves. But I kept wondering what this meeting would be about.

Finally, a day or two before the convention ended, two Reebok executives, David Ropes and Chester Wheeler, brought Dan and Sheri and me together. They had a short videotape they wanted to show us.

What I saw on the screen made my mouth fall open.

It was a series of commercials—in the form of rough sketches—highlighting the rivalry between Dan and me for the '92 Olympic gold medal. Not just two or three commercials but fifteen or twenty of them. "Dan does this. Dave does this. Who is the world's greatest athlete?" Over and over, the same basic idea with a different twist each time, all ending with the words, "To be settled in Barcelona."

This was big. *Man, if they do this,* I thought, *we'll be their main advertising campaign.*

"So what do you think?" David said as he flipped on the lights. "We want to feature you in these commercials. Are you interested?"

Dan and I looked at each other, wide-eyed. Was this really happening? I needed to pinch myself to make sure I wasn't dreaming.

"Well," I said with a grin, "let me think about

Dave Johnson

it." I paused for one second. "Yes." Dan did the same thing.

Then David said that they wanted to run four fifteen-second spots right during the upcoming Super Bowl, the event watched by more people than anything else on TV. We'd need to film the commercials immediately, within the next couple of weeks.

I was amazed that they were really going to invest all this money—twenty-five million dollars in all—in an advertising campaign using Dan and me. It would certainly give the decathlon more visibility in this country than ever before. But even more, I marveled that God was providing this as a way for me to represent him before the world. It would open up many doors for me to talk about my Christian faith.

Dan and I had fun shooting the commercials. It helped us get to know each other better. And the food was great. But let me tell you—it took a lot of work. We completed eleven commercials in ten days, going from sunup to sundown. I was completely exhausted at the end of most days. I couldn't believe all the different people involved—makeup artists, hair stylists, camera and sound crews, producers, directors, people from Reebok and from their ad agency, even caterers. It still amazed me that after twelve hours of shooting, they'd use fifteen or at most thirty seconds of footage for the final product. Dan and I turned the shoots into acting competitions, each trying to finish our part in fewer takes. And of course, each of us thought we were the better actor.

Super Bowl Sunday finally arrived—January 26, 1992—and Sheri and I invited a whole bunch of friends over for a Super Bowl party—or was it a Dan and Dave party? The first spot had baby pictures of Dan and me. The second had photos of us at age four, and the third at age seven. The fourth showed us both competing for the first time. Each time there was the question, "Who is the world's greatest athlete?" Everyone in the house went wild. I called my parents and they were crying for joy because their little boy was on TV.

Every few weeks a new commercial debuted. Newspapers, magazines, and TV shows—not to mention millions of viewers—began to wonder who Dan and Dave were. People started recognizing me when I went places. On the track I would sign hundreds of autographs. I had become one of the best-known athletes in the country.

My friends and "family" at Azusa Pacific University played a key role throughout the whole experience (and to this day) by not letting my head get too big. Most of the people there continued to treat me just as they always had. They kept me humble. Of course they were very excited for me and for the opportunity I would have to tell my story. But they reminded me that no matter how great an athlete I would become, or how short of my goals I would fall, the Lord would love me just the same. He doesn't require me—or anyone—to be the best in the world. All he asks is that I give one hundred percent for him.

Because of my sore knee, I'd hardly trained at all in January and February. But finally the third cortizone injection by the doctor "took" and the pain vanished. For the next six weeks, I worked out long and hard. I got myself in such great shape that in my first meet of the year, the Mt. SAC Relays at Azusa, I actually came within striking distance of the world record. I PR'd in four events and racked up 8727 points, my all-time best. I felt so good and so focused for the entire meet. The score gave me the big boost I needed to carry me into the Trials.

The publicity and the pressure grew in the weeks that followed. Everywhere I went, it seemed, people noticed "that Dave guy" or "that Dan-and-Dave guy." We appeared on magazine covers and on talk shows. People stopped me constantly for autographs and pictures. I wasn't used to this kind of attention, but I tried to concentrate on my training.

Finally the day of the Trials arrived, and Coach Franson, Kevin, and I headed over to Tad Gormley Stadium in New Orleans. It was hot and humid outside—over 90 degrees—and slightly windy. I'd been through two previous Olympic Trials, and knew that my primary task was to relax and earn a spot on the team.

I wasn't prepared for what I saw when we got there. Reebok was handing out thousands of hats, T-shirts, fans, buttons, even pencils and pens—red ones with Dan's name, and blue ones with mine. The crowd, which numbered only a few thousand at first, swelled to more than 17,000 by the end of the day. They were all going wild over the Dan-and-Dave competition.

Dan and I said a brotherly hello to each other before running out on the field. When our names were called, the crowd roared.

I had an average but consistent first day, with a PR in the shot put and a near-PR in the 400. During that race, I was in my final turn when a huge moth flew into my mouth. It startled me, but after six or seven strides I managed to spit it out and still finish strong. Fortunately I had not sucked it in while taking a deep breath. After five events, I was in fifth place, with my best day ahead of me. If I didn't make any mistakes tomorrow, I'd earn my ticket to Barcelona.

Dan had an incredible first day, setting a new world record with his score of 4698. It looked like another showdown between us for the top two spots.

On Day Two, I opened with a shaky but okay hurdle race. Then I threw a solid discus. After seven events, I had moved up to second place behind Dan, who still commanded a 500-point lead.

Then the unexpected happened.

We were preparing to pole vault. During warmups Dan and I both cleared sixteen feet easily. I decided to open at 15'9", a height that I knew would not cause much stress. Dan chose the same. I was nervous, but having been in that situation before, I cleared on my first attempt.

Apparently Dan was feeling much more nervous. He'd been injured early in the season and had not vaulted in a meet all spring. And he'd never been in a situation quite like this before—the pressure of being in the Olympic Trials, with millions watching on TV and millions of your sponsor's dollars riding on your performance.

When he missed on his first attempt, I was

concerned. I saw the lack of confidence in his face, but I still thought he'd recover.

On the second try, he gained enough height, but landed on the bar and knocked it off.

Now I worried. If he didn't clear on this attempt, he'd get zero points for the event and lose his chance to go to Barcelona.

C'mon, Dan, I said to myself as he started down the runway for his final attempt. *I just know you're gonna make it this time.*

But he didn't. As he planted the pole, he hesitated and bailed out before reaching the bar.

I couldn't believe it. So many emotions were racing through my mind. First I was angry at him for altering the Dan-and-Dave plan. What would Reebok do now? What about all the money they were spending, the commercials they still hadn't aired, the publicity they were counting on?

My second thought was, *Wow—it's going to be just my show now. I don't have to worry about Dan beating me. I'm going to win the Trials and the Olympic Games for sure, or at least it'll be a lot easier.*

But then, as I saw him drop to the pit in anguish, I put myself in his Reeboks. I had no-heighted myself several times at the national level. It's the worst feeling in the world, and it happens to nearly all decathletes at some point. But to have it happen at the Olympic Trials must be devastating. I knew how badly he wanted to make this Olympic team. From the very start, I had wanted us both to be in Barcelona. Now a big part of me would be missing there.

I got up and made my way over to him. With tears in my eyes, I put my arms around him and simply said, "I am so sorry, Dan." I truly cared for him and how he must have been feeling. At that moment, I cared very little about myself.

The headlines the next day said, "It's Dave!" I was thrilled to make the team, but it wasn't supposed to turn out this way. Dan wouldn't be at the Games. He belonged there.

Reebok recovered well from the incident. They reaffirmed their commitment to both Dan and me, and in a very classy move, they decided to shoot several new commercials with Dan supporting my road to Barcelona.

As I thought about going to the Games without Dan, I tried to accept that God must have something different in mind for him right now.

I would soon discover that the same was true for me.

10

The Pain in Spain

Besides Dan's elimination from the Olympic team, one other thing cast a shadow over my victory at the Trials: My right ankle hurt afterward. I had felt a pop in it before the Trials but had been able to compete without much difficulty. When I got home and tried to train on it, however, the pain and swelling grew so intense that I had to stop running altogether.

The doctor said it was a bone spur again, but I wasn't convinced, so I went for a special kind of X-ray known as an MRI bone scan. Sure enough, my problem was not a bone spur but a

Dave Johnson

stress fracture in my ankle. What's more, the scan showed that the bone spur I *thought* I had in 1987 when I stepped on the shot had actually been a stress fracture. No wonder it had given me so much pain back then—and now.

I'm not sure who was more upset—Coach or me. When he first told me, there was such despair in his face that I said, "Coach, you look terrible. C'mon, you've gotta help me out here."

"Yeah, I know," he sighed, "I'm just trying to deal with it right now."

I wanted to scream and cry. It wasn't fair. Only three weeks before the start of the Olympic Games. I was favored to win the gold medal.

Coach and I both knew that we'd come too far to stop now. There had to be some kind of reason for this. I was scared to death, but I decided to go for it.

I underwent all kinds of therapy with the doctors and the various machines. I worked out a few times in the swimming pool to maintain my fitness level without putting weight on my foot. I also rode the exercise bike and did some low-impact cross-training.

Early on we decided to keep the whole situation a secret. If I was to do well at the Games—or even finish, for that matter—I would have to maintain the most positive attitude I could muster. I needed to think about my foot as little as possible. So we agreed to tell no more than a handful of our closest friends, so they could pray for us, and of course the necessary medical people. Coach would have to inform the USOC doctors. We also felt it was too risky to tell Reebok or VISA about the injury, because then the news might leak to the press and reporters would be hounding me all the time.

When I arrived in Barcelona, I had only done one running workout since the Trials. I was afraid but ready to do my best. Kevin and Coach gave me nonstop encouragement.

"Hey, you're still in great shape, Dave," they'd say. "You're gonna do just fine. You can still win the whole thing."

Mentally, I knew I could win. I knew I could even break the world record. The main question was whether my foot would hold up.

I woke up on the morning of the first day of competition and carefully stepped out of bed. I knew the pounding my foot was about to take. I was afraid of injuring it worse so that I would never run again. Afraid of failing in front of so many people. Afraid of disappointing all my friends and relatives who were part of my Olympic dream.

The stadium was mostly empty at 9 A.M.

when we lined up for the 100 meters. After two false starts, we finally took off. It felt great to let my body give one hundred percent again. Halfway through the race, however, I felt a stabbing pain in my foot, so sharp that I slowed up a bit to relieve it. My time of 11.16 was only average, and I needed above-average scores if I was to win. Looking up at the replay of the race on the stadium monitors, I could tell I was already favoring my right leg, but no one seemed to notice.

Coach Franson and Kevin stopped down to offer encouragement before the long jump. My distance was just over 24 feet— good, considering the speed I was losing on the approach.

During the shot put I had a major scare. My foot was holding up okay so far. On my first throw, it hurt as I began, hurt when I uncoiled and released, then hurt again as I stopped myself. But not too bad. The official called a foul, however. Then, on my second throw, the red flag went up again. Neither one felt like a foul to me.

Now things were getting serious. *Relax, it's okay,* I said to myself, *you still have another throw. No one fouls three throws.* A third foul would mean zero points, and I'd be out of contention.

When my final turn came, I probably threw a little more cautiously just to make sure I was legal. But when I looked over at the official, he raised the red flag yet again.

No way!

I'd just been called for my third foul. I was out. Pack up and go home. But I just knew I hadn't stepped on top of the toeboard. I knew I'd made a legal throw. I went back into the ring and stood there, demanding an explanation.

"Hey, come and show me how I fouled," I said. "Show me what you saw. Do you speak English? Please show me what you saw."

The guy just stood there, not knowing what to do. And I refused to budge until somebody would talk to me. On the inside, I was nearly panicking. *There is no way I'm going to get this to go in my favor. Officials don't make mistakes at the Games. What am I going to do? It's over. This is hopeless.*

Then the head official came over and spoke with the flag man in Spanish. A couple of others joined the discussion. Then I saw my throw being replayed three or four times on the big screen while the officials watched. Maybe I still had a chance.

Finally the ruling came through from the head official: I had not fouled, after all. And since no measurement had been taken of my third throw, I'd be given a fourth attempt—something unheard of in the Olympics. It was a miracle.

Of course, I still needed to make a legal throw. As I nervously stepped back into the ring, the Spanish crowd booed and whistled in disapproval.

Lord, help me with this, I prayed, trying to stop shaking. *I've never had to compete with the crowd against me before. Give me your strength, and help me to relax.*

I relaxed. I got myself set. Then I unleashed the biggest throw of my life—50'1". A PR by nearly a foot. *YEAH!*

The shot heard round the world.

The booing grew louder as I left the stadium for the siesta break. Coach and Kevin were waiting for me, breathless over what had just happened. Sheri gave me a big kiss. And Bruce Jenner congratulated me in the tunnel.

"Boy, you were lucky, Dave," he said. Maybe, but I think it was more than luck. It was the Lord announcing to the world that a story was beginning to unfold.

Since the high jump would not start until 5:30, we returned to the hotel to relax a little. I knew it would not be easy to finish on my ankle, which was beginning to swell. I was well off the pace for a world record but still believed I had a good chance for the gold. I had to trust that the Lord was in control.

Back at the stadium, I had difficulty with the high jump. My legs were tired—the right one from the injury, and the left one from working harder to compensate. As a result, both my speed and my steps were off. When the jumping finally ended nearly four hours later, I had only managed 6'6"—okay, but well short of what I needed.

Under the lights and a near-capacity crowd, we lined up for the first heat of the 400 at about 9:30. At the gun, I gave every ounce I had, with no attempt to conserve energy. I ran well until the last 100 meters, when the ankle pain and leg fatigue took over. I finished a full second slower than my average.

For the most part, I'd been able to mask the pain of my injury that first day. I probably looked normal to the announcers, TV viewers, even the other athletes. But after the 400, people began to wonder why I wasn't in peak form. Reporters were starting to ask questions. At first I just brushed them off, but then I realized I needed to give some kind of explanation.

"Yes, there is something going on," I finally told them, without going into any detail. "I need to evaluate it overnight, and I'll let you know tomorrow after the hurdles."

I was in ninth place after five events, about 280 points out of first. I had trailed Dan by more than that on two previous occasions and still come back to win. But that was on a healthy foot. Back in my hotel room, my battered, swollen foot hurt more than ever. As I lay there in bed, I felt angry that God was letting this happen to me. Why would he not want a gold medal to shine in my life for him? The Olympic Games was the perfect place for me to make an impact for Christ, especially after the Reebok publicity. Tears welled up as I realized I had been preparing myself for tomorrow for ten years, only to be stuck with this injury.

The Lord must have heard my questioning, because I began to feel a little reassured. It was as if he was saying to me, *Don't worry, Dave. I haven't left you out in the cold. I'm still right here with you. I love you, and I'm still working in your life. Just keep on trusting me.*

As much as I wanted that gold medal, maybe he was trying to tell me that something else was even more important. I remembered the goal he had first helped me to set—to take on the decathlon and all of life as Christ would. That goal hadn't changed—medal or no medal.

In spite of the pain, in spite of the disappointment, I could aim for that goal with complete confidence.

I woke up very stiff the next morning, stiffer than usual because my whole body—especially my left leg—had been working overtime to compensate for my right ankle, which throbbed even before I got out of bed.

As I warmed up for the hurdles, I tried to figure out what to tell the reporters. I had told them I'd answer their questions after this event. I knew that if anything would completely break my foot, it would be the hurdles. I would have to kick and come down ten times on that fractured bone with all my weight.

I barely survived. After the third or fourth hurdle, my foot popped again, and I nearly screamed in pain but hung on for a 14.76 finish. X-rays after the games would show that the stress fracture had split further. *Okay, more pain,* I thought as I sat down. *That's just great. Now what's going to happen?* Franson came down to see how I felt.

"Look," he said, "the next event's the discus. It's not going to hurt to throw the discus."

With an ice pack on my ankle, I talked to the reporters who had clustered around me. "I've been competing on a stress fracture to the right

Dave Johnson

foot," I explained. "The injury first occurred two weeks before the Trials." I didn't have time to say much more than that. I figured I'd throw the discus and then call it a meet.

Amid continued boos from the crowd, I had a fine throw of more than 161 feet. But then I wondered: Was the Lord trying to tell me I was strong enough to keep going?

My foot felt worse now. To continue would risk injuring it still further. And if the physical pain wasn't bad enough, the emotional pain of not reaching my goals had begun to set in. I would not break the world record; I would not win the gold medal; and the way my foot was feeling, I wouldn't win any medal at all. What reason did I have to finish?

I talked it over with Coach and Kevin during the siesta break. I was trying to get them to say, "Well, okay, don't finish," but they never would. Instead, their response was, "Why not just give it a try and see what happens?"

The pole vault frightened me even more than the hurdles. I worried that I wouldn't gain sufficient speed on my foot. If you run too slowly, the pole can whip you in the wrong direction and cause you to miss the pit completely. I cleared a couple of heights during warm-ups, but by the time the official vaulting began, my ankle was so swollen that I could hardly tie my shoe. And the pain was almost impossible to block out.

At one point while I prepared to make my approach, the picture of Jesus Christ carrying his cross came to mind. He had endured incredible pain, but had never given up. I tried to think of my vaulting pole as a cross, and because of what Christ had done for me, I told myself I wouldn't give up, either. I got so inspired that I reached all the way to 16'8", even though my foot was hurting worse.

But when the bar went up to 17', the pain simply became unbearable after two limping attempts and I lost it. Angrily I threw down the pole and stormed off the field, leaving my gear behind. I was through.

Coach Franson and Kevin met me in the training room under the stadium. Utterly broken, I dropped into a chair and dissolved into tears. This isn't how the Olympic Games were supposed to be. I simply couldn't go on. I had nothing left to give. I couldn't handle any more pain or any more disappointment. I just wanted to get out of there.

In a caring but firm way, Coach told me that the most important thing now was for me to finish this meet and leave the results up to God.

Dave Johnson

"Dave, I don't know what the pain feels like," he said. "I know that it's got to be so hard for you. But I'm your coach, and I'm saying that we can finish this."

"I don't think so," I complained.

"Well, I *do* think so." As he spoke, I could see the tears in his own eyes. He loved me and cared about me like a father. But even more, he believed in me and in God's greater purpose for my life. He put his arms around me and for a few minutes we cried together.

At this point I had to have some kind of painkiller if I was going to finish. So Coach brought in one of the doctors to evaluate my foot and give me an injection. He inserted the needle down through the top of my foot, hoping to deaden the area around the fractured bone.

But when I went back out to throw the javelin, the shot didn't work. It did nothing for the pain and only made my foot harder to control. I lost my footing and nearly fell on the first throw, which landed far short. For the second attempt, I played it safe by taking six or seven steps before throwing instead of my usual run-up. The toss went far enough to lift me from sixth place into third—making me a silver- or bronze-medal contender. Because of another error by the officials, I didn't get to take a third throw.

While I stumbled through the javelin competition, Coach Franson watched and cheered me on from a nearby section of the stands. An American boy, probably ten or eleven years old, saw him yelling to me, and came up alongside him.

"Is that Dave?" the boy said.

"Yeah." Coach was pretty upset himself, and didn't really feel like talking.

"Dave's gonna win, huh?" said the boy.

"No, I don't think so."

"How come? Isn't he from the Dan-and-Dave commercials?"

"Yeah, but he's got a broken foot. He broke it just before coming here."

The boy's eyes widened. "Really? Then what's he doing out there? How can he do that stuff on a broken foot?"

"Because he wants to do his very best. He's an American, and this is the Olympics. He's not going to give up. You know what? Dave's still out there because of kids just like you. As you get older, you're gonna have times when you want to give up and quit, and that's when you can think of Dave. Even though he's not going to win, he's gonna finish because of kids like you."

Down on the field, I wanted to give up and quit.

Dave Johnson

After the javelin disaster, I told the doctors that the shot didn't help. Coach and Kevin joined me as they decided to give one more injection. This time, while I lay on the examining table, they stuck the needle straight up through my arch. Words can't describe the pain I felt as the doctor moved the needle around to apply medication in different areas. It hurt more than the stress fracture itself, and I couldn't control my tears. Everything came rushing out at once—the pain, the anger, the fear, the despair. I asked Franson if I should quit. I asked Kevin if I should quit. I asked God if I should quit.

"Dave," Coach said, "I think this whole thing is way bigger than you and I even realize. I just got done talking with a boy who thinks you're the greatest thing in the world because you're out there competing on a broken foot." He went on to tell me about his conversation.

"You've got to believe, Dave, that God is allowing an incredible story to unfold through this Olympic Games. It's not the story we thought it would be, and it may not have the same audience you'd have if you'd won the gold medal with all its glamor and glory. It's a story about lots and lots of people who've stood behind you. It's about a dream, a disappointment, and then about not giving up. You know the Olympics is not really about winning gold medals; it's about doing your very best before the world."

We all cried some more. Maybe Coach was right. Maybe something bigger was going on that I didn't understand. Maybe God wanted me to learn that greatness was not so much about being the best, but about *doing* my best. Not so much about winning as about enduring when the going gets tough.

Coach, Kevin, and I prayed together for strength to make it through the 1500 meters— one metric mile. I stepped down from the table, but I couldn't tell my foot had hit the floor. The bottom was completely numb. And as I tried to jog on it, I still felt pain. It was hopeless. How could I run safely if I couldn't feel the ground under me? I'd land on it wrong and completely break off my foot, like race-horses sometimes do.

"I can't go out there," I said. "I'll be an embarrassment to my country."

"Embarrassment?" Coach said. "That would be the *last* thing anyone would say about you. You're going out and overcoming the odds. It's hard enough for an athlete to get here at all, and you've not only gotten here, but you might actually win a bronze medal in spite of this injury. You've already performed this decathlon at a world-class level on a broken foot. Dave, you've *got* to run. You've got to finish this."

Pulling myself together, I determined to make it through this last event. My group lined up under the stadium lights at about 10 P.M. At the gun, I almost fell but caught myself and managed to establish a rhythm, though my right foot dragged. I had to look down every now and then to see if it was landing properly. It felt so strange—numb on the bottom, painful on the top.

After the first lap I thought, *Okay, I can stop now—I gave it a try.* But something in me said to keep going. The crowd was screaming—mostly for their own decathletes, but it gave me extra energy.

At 800 meters, I said, *You're halfway there now—you might as well keep running.* At this point medals no longer mattered; I just wanted to finish. Adrenaline must have kicked in for the rest of the race, because I felt less pain in my foot. I was actually able to pick up a little speed at the end.

It was over. I had finished. I had won the bronze medal. And thanks to Coach Franson, Kevin, Sheri, my parents, my friends, and especially the Lord, I had survived.

Faith for the Future

Life since the Barcelona Games has turned out to be extremely busy, in spite of taking the entire year of 1993 off (from competition, at least). Surgeons repaired the bone in my foot with a couple of screws, and I decided to give it a year to heal completely. But now I'm back to training again for the '96 Olympic Games. Barring injury or some other unforeseen circumstances, I intend to be there, duking it out with Dan for the gold medal.

Along with my training, I've been able to tell my story and share my faith with students from elementary school through college. I encourage kids to stay in school and go for their dreams. I've participated in school assemblies for the D.A.R.E. program (Drug and Alcohol Recognition Education), where I speak out against the use of alcohol, drugs, and steroids. I tell people I am living proof that one can reach the highest levels of athletic performance without using steroids.

On one occasion I got to meet Billy Graham and speak at his Portland, Oregon, crusade.

Dave Johnson

Another time I stood before a packed-out stadium during a San Diego Chargers vs. San Francisco 49'ers pre-season game and spoke on behalf of the U.S. Olympic Committee.

I've had some fun, too. I've played in a number of golf tournaments, including ones sponsored by Michael Jordan and Magic Johnson. And for the past two years I was invited to the annual Jeep Superstars competition, in which celebrity athletes from all different sports battle it out in areas that are not their specialty, such as kayaking, swimming, cycling, running an obstacle course, and so on. The proceeds go to charity, and the winner gets to drive off in a new Jeep Grand Cherokee.

The '93 competition took place in Cancun, Mexico (hey, somebody had to go), and I actually won the whole thing against the likes of Hershel Walker, Evander Holyfield, and other star athletes. In this year's showdown, held in Waikiki, Hawaii, the prize had increased to two Jeeps, and—you guessed it—I took first place again. What a riot.

You know, I ended up learning much more about life by not winning that gold medal. If I'd won the gold, I might be saying something different to kids around the country. I might be saying, "Hey, it's great at the top—and maybe if you try hard enough, you can be just like me. Then you can sit back and enjoy fame and fortune."

Instead, I'm able to say something much more realistic and hopeful. Yes, we should set our sights high and go for our goals and dreams with all our heart—just as I am still going for mine. We should believe in the talents God has given us and strive to give nothing less than one hundred percent of ourselves. We should "kick major booty" and hang in there when the going gets tough.

But even more important than reaching the goal or realizing the dream is the kind of person we've become along the way. That person is what God cares about most.

And that's what "aiming high" is really all about.